# BASIC GOALS IN SPELLING

**Sixth Edition**

William Kottmeyer & Audrey Claus

**Webster Division, McGraw-Hill Book Company**

New York    St. Louis    San Francisco    Dallas    Atlanta

William Kottmeyer has served in the St. Louis Public Schools as teacher, principal, reading specialist, and superintendent. A nationally recognized educational innovator, Dr. Kottmeyer has created a wide variety of basic language-skills materials. Currently author-in-residence in the Webster Division, his publications include *Basic Goals in Spelling, Basic Goals in Reading, The Webster Reading Centers,* the *+4 Reading Booster, Decoding and Meaning,* the *+10 Vocabulary Booster,* the *Classroom Reading Clinic, Dr. Spello,* and the *Everyreader Series.*

Audrey Claus has served in the St. Louis Public Schools as teacher, consultant, elementary principal, and curriculum coordinator. Presently author-in-residence in the Webster Division, Miss Claus is co-author of *Basic Goals in Spelling, Basic Goals in Reading,* and the *+10 Vocabulary Booster.*

**Sponsoring Editor:** Richard Paul
**Editing Supervisor:** Mary Lewis Wang
**Designer:** Richard O'Leary
**Production Manager:** Tom Goodwin

The illustrations in this book were created by Buck Brown, Tom Dunnington, Sally Springer, Joseph Veno, Jack Wallen, and Gordon Willman.
The cover design is by E. Rohne Rudder.

Library of Congress Cataloging in Publication Data

Kottmeyer, William, date.
    Basic goals in spelling.

    SUMMARY: An eight-volume elementary spelling series
which presents linguistic principles and coordinates
the encoding and decoding skills of spelling and reading.
    1. Spellers. [1. Spellers] I. Claus, Audrey,
date. joint author. II. Title.
PE1145.2.K6 1980            428'.1            79-224
ISBN 0-07-034363-2 (v. 3)

# Table of Contents

# How To Write The Alphabet

a b c d e f g h i

j k l m n o p q r

s t u v w x y z

A B C D E F G H I

J K L M N O P Q R

S T U V W X Y Z

a b c d e f g h i

j k l m m o p q r

s t u v w x y z

A B C D E F G H I

J K L M N O P Q R

S T U V W X Y Z

v

# Sounds and Letters

Each of these consonant letters spells the starting sound of the key-picture word in the box.

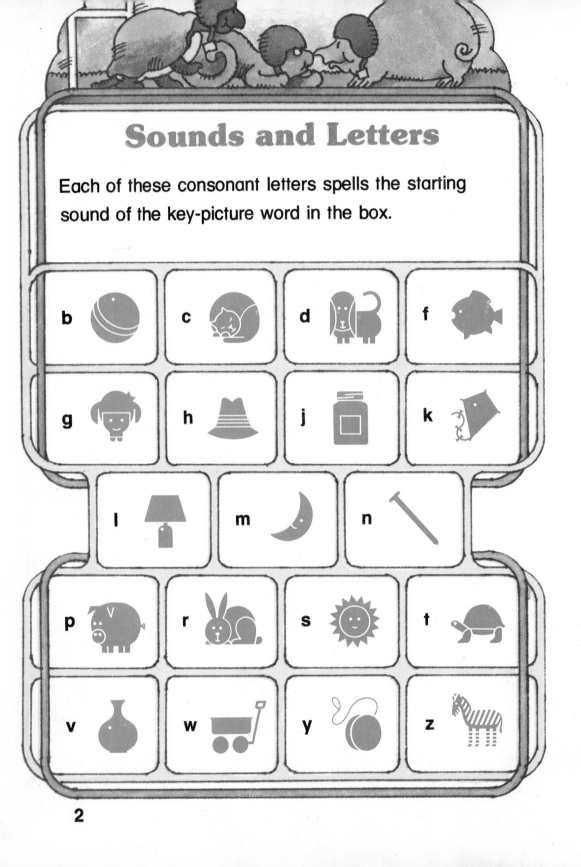

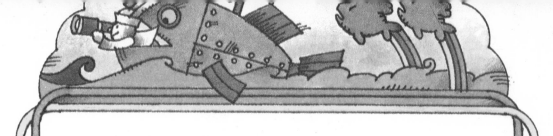

Write the consonant letters that start the key-picture words.

1.    2.    3.

4.    5.    6.

7.    8.    9.

10.    11.    12.

13.    14.    15.

16.    17.    18.

19.

# 1 Short-Vowel Words

| | | | | |
|---|---|---|---|---|
| glad | wet | trip | hunt | drop |
| stamp | best | fix | dug | spot |
| plant | kept | list | just | cost |

▽ front

The words in the spelling list have short-vowel sounds.

The short **a** sound is the  sound in **glad**.

The short **e** sound is the sound in **wet**.

The short **i** sound is the sound in **trip**.

The short **u** sound is the sound in **hunt**.

The short **o** sound is the sound in **drop** or

the sound in **cost**.

4

**1.** Say the short-vowel words. Hear the sounds.

**2.** Write the words in which **a** spells the short **a** sound.

**3.** Write the words in which **e** spells the short **e** sound and the words in which **i** spells the short **i** sound.

**4.** Write the words in which **o** spells the short **o** sound and the words in which **u** spells the short **u** sound.

> A **snurk** is a word that is not spelled the way it sounds.
>
> Say **front.** What short-vowel sound do you hear? Why do we call **front** a snurk?

**5.** Write **front, just,** and **cost.** Draw a line under the word with the 🦩 sound.

## Working with the Word List

**1.** Write the words that end with the 🐷 sound.

**2.** Write **hunt, cost, kept,** and **fix.** Draw a line under the words that have the same starting sound.

5

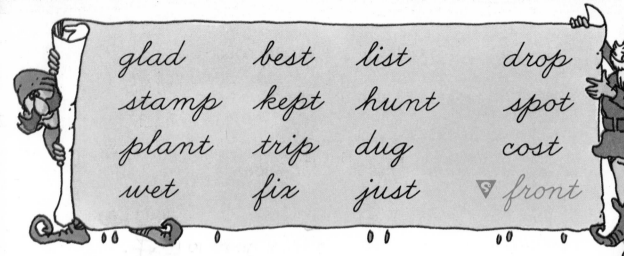

glad  best  list   drop

stamp kept hunt  spot

plant  trip  dug   cost

wet  fix   just   front

**3.** Write **dug, drop, glad,** and **best.** Draw a line under the word that starts with the 🔵 sound.

**4.** Write the word for each meaning.

 **a.** let slip   **b.** mend   **c.** not back

**5.** Use five of these words to write a sentence. Put the period at the end.

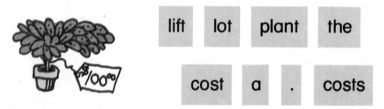

| lift | lot | plant | the |
|------|-----|-------|-----|

| cost | a | . | costs |
|------|---|---|-------|

**6.** Use five of these words to write a sentence.

| his | best | got | hat |
|-----|------|-----|-----|

| hunt | . | glad | wet |
|------|---|------|-----|

6

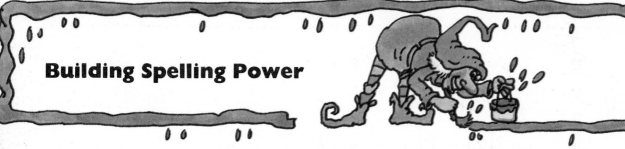

# Building Spelling Power

**1.** Change the short-vowel spellings to make new words. Write the new words.

**a.** Change **trip** to  . **b.** Change **fix** to  .

**c.** Change **dug** to  . **d.** Change **stamp** to  .

**2.** Change the starting sounds to make new words. Write the new words.

**a.** Change **lift** to  . **b.** Change **trip** to  .

**c.** Change **cost** to  . **d.** Change **just** to  .

/a/ stands for the vowel sound in **glad.**
/e/ stands for the vowel sound in **wet.**
/i/ stands for the vowel sound in **trip.**
/o/ stands for the vowel sound in **drop.**
/ô/ stands for the vowel sound in **cost.**
/u/ stands for the vowel sound in **hunt.**

# Spelling Helps Reading

Sound out these short-vowel words.

| | | | | | | |
|---|---|---|---|---|---|---|
| back | swept | box | belt | bus | cut | camp |
| slept | drag | drum | dust | flag | fox | gift |
| hand | log | nest | job | six | tent | crop |
| lamp | melt | next | rock | frog | test | twins |

Write the **B** word that belongs with the **A** words.

| **A** | | | **B** | | |
|---|---|---|---|---|---|
| 1. leg | hip | neck | grand | hand | risk |
| 2. hat | belt | sock | pin | slot | cap |
| 3. sled | blocks | top | drum | log | pig |
| 4. pot | tub | pan | jug | plant | flap |
| 5. frog | cat | fox | tent | nest | dog |
| 6. bed | lamp | rug | mop | desk | bus |
| 7. jump | run | hop | sit | skip | rest |
| 8. milk | buns | crust | tin | ham | bug |
| 9. Fred | Ben | Dan | Sam | Peg | Nan |
| 10. stamp | camp | damp | stump | limp | tramp |

We hear the sound and write the letter.
It makes us spell short-vowel words better.
Ah, how nice this spelling works,
If we keep track of all the snurks!

8

# 2 Pass the Eggs Words

| | | | | |
|---|---|---|---|---|
| add | less | stiff | doll | cuff |
| pass | spell | spill | toss | buzz |
| class | egg | kiss | odd | dull |

We sometimes use the same two consonant letters to spell one consonant sound.

**ss** spells the  sound in **pass.**

**ll** spells the sound in **spill.**

**dd** spells the sound in **add.**

**ff** spells the sound in **stiff.**

**zz** spells the sound in **buzz.**

**gg** spells the sound in **egg.**

9

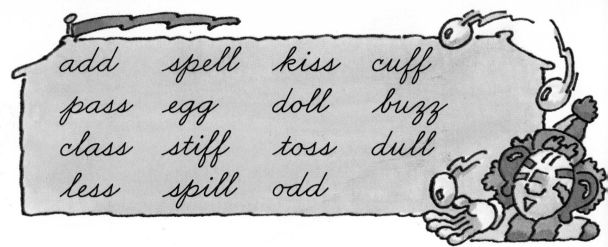

add　　spell　　kiss　　cuff
pass　　egg　　doll　　buzz
class　　stiff　　toss　　dull
less　　spill　　odd

**1.** Write the spelling words that end with the  sound. Draw a line under each **ll**.

**2.** Write the words that end with the ☺ sound.

**3.** Write the words that end with **gg, zz,** and **ff.**

**4.** Write a spelling word for each picture.

a. 　　b.　　c.

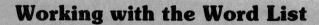

## Working with the Word List

**1.** Write the words with the /a/ sound.

**2.** Write the words with the /o/ sound. Draw a line under each vowel letter.

**10**

**3.** Write the words with the /i/ sound. Draw a line under each vowel letter.

**4.** Write the words with the /u/ sound. Draw a line under each vowel letter.

**5.** Write the words with the /e/ sound. Draw a line under each vowel letter.

**6.** Write a spelling word with the **ing** ending for each of these pictures.

a.          b.          c.

**7.** Add **s** to three words to spell "more than one."

a.          b.          c.

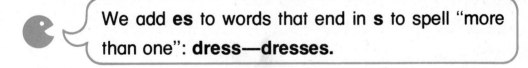

We add **es** to words that end in **s** to spell "more than one": **dress—dresses.**

**8.** Write the words that spell "more than one" **class** and "more than one" **kiss.**

11

## Building Spelling Power

Write the words for each picture. Draw a line under each word that ends with the same two consonant letters.

1. an odd brass bell

   an add brass bell

2. some glass on a hill

   some grass on a hill

3. a cross on a doll dress

   a cross on a dull dress

/d/ stands for the sound that ends **add**.
/g/ stands for the sound that ends **egg**.
/l/ stands for the sound that ends **still**.
/f/ stands for the sound that ends **stiff**.
/s/ stands for the sound that ends **pass**.
/z/ stands for the sound that ends **buzz**.

## Spelling Helps Reading

Sound out these Pass the Eggs words.

| bell | boss | brass | cliff | cross | dress | fell |
|------|------|-------|-------|-------|-------|------|
| bill | fill | loss | puff | glass | grass | hill |
| inn | mill | miss | swell | off | muff | sell |
| skull | sniff | ill | still | tell | well | smell |

Some words tell what we do. We call them **verbs.** Some words are the names of things. We call them **nouns.**

Read the four words in each row. Write three nouns or three verbs in each row.

1. bell    cliff    glass    spin
2. add    fell    flag    fill
3. grass    eggs    lift    hill
4. hop    pill    doll    skull
5. gift    sell    sniff    spell
6. mill    jump    class    moss
7. muff    nest    dog    melt
8. lamp    tell    dig    sit
9. spill    job    snip    skip
10. drip    beg    tent    kill

# 3 Stop-Stopped-Stopping Words

grab   step   drip   stop   rub

plan   pet   skip   trot   scrub

drag   beg   slip   rob   hug

When a word ends with one vowel letter and one consonant letter, we double the last consonant letter before we add **ed** or **ing**.

stop   stopped   stopping

hug   hugged   hugging

**1.** Say the spelling words. Hear the ending sounds.

**2.** Write the words with the /a/ sound and the /u/ sound.

14

**3.** Write the words with the /i/ sound and the words with the /o/ sound.

**4.** Write the words with the /e/ sound.

**5.** Write **rob, pet,** and **rub** with **ing** endings.

**6.** Write **skip, hug,** and **scrub** as **ed** words.

## Working with the Word List

**1.** Write a verb, or "doing word," for each picture. Then write each word with its **ing** ending.

a.      b.      c.

**2.** Write a verb, or "doing word," for each picture. Then write each word with its **ed** ending.

a.      b.      c.

*grab  pet  slip  rub*
*plan  beg  stop  scrub*
*drag  drip  trot  hug*
*step  skip  rob*

**3.** Write the word for each meaning.

    **a.** ask        **b.** run        **c.** pat

> When a word ends with two consonant letters, we do not double the last letter before we add **ed** or **ing: plant, planted, planting.**

**4.** Write **rest, plan,** and **skip** with **ing** endings.

**5.** Use four of the words to make a sentence. Put the period at the end.

| have | stepped | Jeff | stopped |
| . | digging | has | begging |

We can use the sounds of key picture words to spell new words.

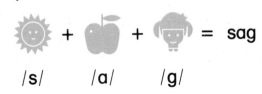

/s/     /a/     /g/

**1.** Write new words. Then write each word with the **ed** and the **ing** endings.

a. 🎩 + ☂ + 🌙 = ____.

b. ☀ + 🐢 + 🐘 + 🐷 = ____.

c. 🛒 + 🍎 + 👧 = ____.

**2.** Write the word for the space in the sentence. Then write the two snurks in the sentence.

Nell and Bill have been ____.

/b/ stands for the sound that starts **beg.**

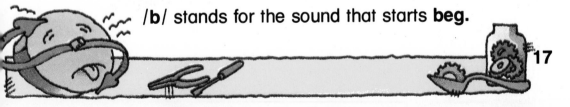

17

Sound out these Stopped-Stopping words.

| | | | | |
|---|---|---|---|---|
| begged | getting | planning | stripped | tapped |
| clapped | grabbed | robbed | sitting | stepped |
| cutting | hopping | running | stopped | stopping |
| digging | hugging | scrubbed | slipped | swimming |
| dropped | hummed | setting | spinning | skipping |

How many **p**'s in **hop?** In **hopping?**
In **shop** and **chop?** In **shopping, chopping?**
**Mop** and **mopping? Drop** and **dropping?**
Words like these need more than **ing.**
Words like these must have a **ping!**

Count the **p**'s in **dip** and **dipping,**
**Rip** and **ripping, tip** and **tipping,**
**Slip** and **slipping, drip** and **dripping.**
They simply will not stand for **ing.**
Every one must have a **ping!**

You may **tap,** but I am **tapping.**
He may **clap,** but she is **clapping.**
We may **slap,** but they are **slapping.**
It will not do to add just **ing.**
The **p**'s are free, so add the **ping!**

# 4  Which Fresh Thing Words

which  splash  path  strong  branch

when  fresh,  tenth  swing  inch

whip  shot  thump  thing  chest

§ sure

**Which Fresh Thing** words have two-letter consonant sounds.

**wh** spells the sounds that start **which.**

**ch** spells the sound that ends **which.**

**sh** spells the sound that ends **fresh.**

**th** spells the sound that starts **thing.**

**ng** spells the sound that ends **thing.**

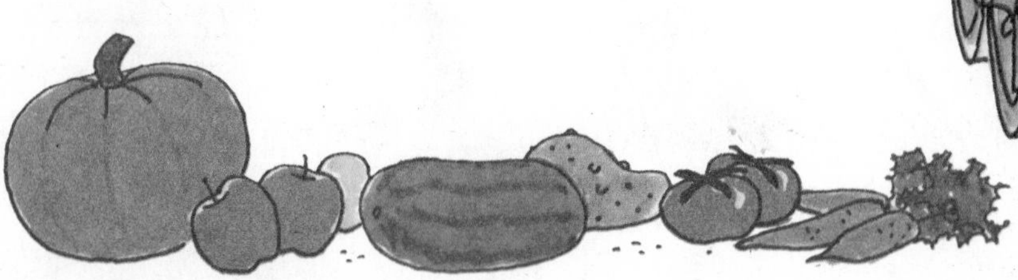

**1.** Write the words with /a/ and with /i/. Draw lines under the letters that spell two-letter consonant sounds.

**19**

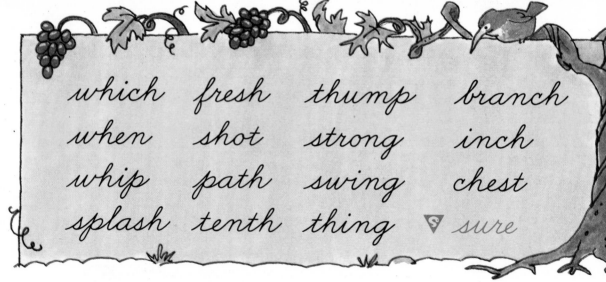

*which    fresh    thump    branch*
*when     shot     strong   inch*
*whip     path     swing    chest*
*splash   tenth    thing    sure*

**2.** Write the words with /e/ and with /u/. Draw lines under the letters that spell two-letter consonant sounds.

**3.** Write **shot, strong,** and **sure.** Draw lines under the words that start with the  sound.

 Say **sure.** Does **s** spell /s/? Does **u** spell /u/? Why do we call **sure** a snurk?

## Working with the Word List

**1.** Write the word for each picture.

a.

b.

c.

**2.** Read the sentences. Write each word under the sign that shows its vowel sound. The signs are /a/, /e/, /i/, and /o/ or /ô/. Do not write **the, a,** or the snurk.

This swing hangs on a strong branch.

Beth and Bob have stepped off the path.

That chest is six inches long.

Fred has dropped his fresh eggs.

**3.** Write a snurk to fit the space in the sentence.

They are _____ of winning.

**4.** Write the word for each meaning.

**a.** box with a    **b.** hit with    **c.** hit with
big lid              the fist           a strap

**d.** way made      **e.** not weak    **f.** at what
for walking                             time

# Building Spelling Power

**1.** Write new **ch** words.

a.  + + + **ch** = _____ .

b. + + + **ch** = _____ .

c. + + + **ch** = _____ .

**2.** Use all the words to write sentences.

a.

| The | to | have |
|-----|-----|------|

| wants | . | lunch | king |
|-------|---|-------|------|

b.

| has | lots | fun | . | Pat |
|-----|------|-----|---|-----|

| the | on | of | ranch |
|-----|-----|-----|-------|

/**sh**/ stands for the sound that ends **fresh.**

/**hw**/ stands for the sounds that start **which.**

/**ch**/ stands for the sound that ends **which.**

/**th**/ stands for the sound that starts **thing.**

/**ng**/ stands for the sound that ends **thing.**

22

# Spelling Helps Reading

Sound out these Which Fresh Thing words.

| bath | dish | ranch | swung | chin | length |
|------|------|-------|-------|------|--------|
| cloth | moth | spring | chill | king | whiz |
| lunch | sixth | bunch | hang | ship | wings |
| shop | brush | flash | shelf | shell | rush |
| bench | fish | rang | thrill | chop | fifth |

**1.** One noun in each line does not belong with the other three. Find that word and write it.

**a.** whips     branches     inches     chest

**b.** things     paths     bench     baths

**c.** chin     dishes     brushes     bunches

**d.** flashes     kings     moth     lunches

**e.** ranch     ship     wings     shop

**2.** One verb in each line does not belong with the other three. Find that word and write it.

**a.** splashed     thumped     swung     swing

**b.** chilled     chopped     fished     hang

**c.** rang     ring     flashed     whizzed

**d.** sing     brush     rush     sang

**e.** sprang     spring     blush     sting

# 5 Quick Pink Witch Words

| | | | |
|---|---|---|---|
| clock | wink | hatch | quick |
| trick | drink | itch | quit |
| kick | drank | scratch | quack |
| block | skunk | switch | quiet |

**Quick Pink Witch** words have tricky consonant letters.

**qu** spells the  sounds that start **quick.**

**ck** spells the  sound that ends **quick.**

**n** before **k** spells the ⭕ sound in **pink.**

**tch** spells the  sound that ends **witch.**

**1.** Write the six words that end with **ck.** Draw a line under each **ck.**

**2.** Write the words with the /ng/ sound. Draw a line under each **nk.** Circle the word with the /u/ sound.

Say **quiet.** Hear two word parts, or **syllables.**
How is **quiet** different from the other **qu** words?
Why do we call **quiet** a snurk?

**3.** Write **quit, quick,** and **quiet.** Draw a line under each word with the /i/ sound.

**4.** Write **sure, front,** and **quiet.** Circle the word with the /u/ sound. Draw a line under the word that means "still."

**5.** Write the four words that end with the /ch/ sound. Draw a line under each **tch.**

## Working with the Word List

**1.** Write the word for each picture. Circle the words with the /o/ sound.

a.

b.

c.

clock   wink   hatch      quick
trick   drink   itch       quit
kick   drank   scratch   quack
block   skunk   switch   quiet

**2.** Write the word for each meaning.

   **a.** tickly feeling   **b.** shut one eye   **c.** fast

**3.** Write each picture word with **ed** and **ing** endings.

**a.**    **b.**   **c.**

**4.** The word **quit** ends with one consonant letter. Write **quit.**
Then write **quit** with its **ing** ending.

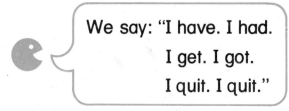

We say: "I have. I had.
        I get. I got.
        I quit. I quit."

**5.** Write a spelling word to fit the space in the sentence.

   I got a glass of milk and ____ it.

26

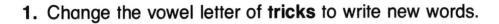

**1.** Change the vowel letter of **tricks** to write new words.

a.      b.

**2.** Change the starting letters of **drank** to write new words.

a.      b.

**3.** Use two of these words to tell about each picture: **ducks, hatching, clocks, catching, quilts, chicks, matching, skunks, ticking, quacking.**

a.      b.

c.      d.

**/k/** stands for the sound that starts and ends **kick.**

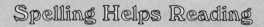

# Spelling Helps Reading

Sound out these Quick Pink Witch words.

| think | hitch | quilt | tick | chunk | pack |
| crutch | pink | stretch | chick | match | sock |
| patch | stick | catch | lock | shrink | witch |
| squint | black | lick | sank | truck | clock |
| thank | honk | quiz | track | crack | sink |

Read the five words in each line. Write the four words that belong together.

1. plank    stick    truck    branch    match
2. mink    cat    skunk    rat    dock
3. chick    deck    duck    hen    thrush
4. honk    cluck    quack    lock    clank
5. black    tan    back    pink    red
6. Jack    Frank    Nell    socks    Dick
7. lick    suck    drink    sip    sit
8. pitch    catch    bat    run    pet
9. tank    crutch    glass    cup    crock
10. quilt    quiz    quick    kick    squint

# 6 Play Train Game Words

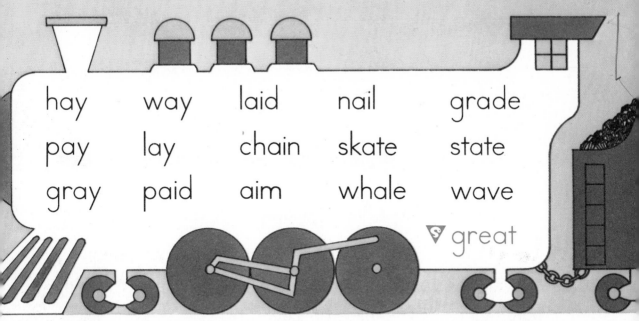

| | | | | |
|---|---|---|---|---|
| hay | way | laid | nail | grade |
| pay | lay | chain | skate | state |
| gray | paid | aim | whale | wave |
| | | | | ★ great |

The vowel sound in **Play Train Game** words is called the long **a** sound.

**ay** spells the long **a** sound in **play**.

**ai** spells the long **a** sound in **train**.

**a**-consonant letter-**e** spells the long **a** sound in **game**.

1. Say the spelling words. Hear the vowel sounds.

2. Write the words in which **ay** spells the vowel sound.

29

hay    lay    aim    grade

pay    paid    nail    state

gray    laid    skate    wave

way    chain    whale    great

**3.** Write the words in which **ai** spells the vowel sound. Circle the word that means "put down."

**4.** Write the words that have **a**-consonant letter-**e.** Circle the word that means "to glide on ice."

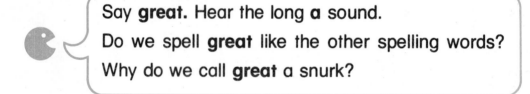

Say **great.** Hear the long **a** sound.
Do we spell **great** like the other spelling words?
Why do we call **great** a snurk?

**5.** Write **great** and the other spelling words that start with the same two consonant sounds as **great.**

**6.** Write **front, great,** and **sure.** Draw a line under the word with the /sh/ sound.

**7.** Write **skate, chain,** and **great.** Draw lines under the two words that rhyme.

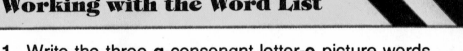

# Working with the Word List

1. Write the three **a**-consonant letter-**e** picture words.

a.      b.      c.

2. Write a word for each of these starting sounds.

   **a.** /ch/        **b.** /hw/        **c.** /s/

   **d.** /s/         **e.** /l/         **f.** /l/

3. Use the words to write two sentences.

| paid | skate | Ann | and |
|------|-------|-----|-----|
| . | to | Dave | have |

| to | pay | . | Ray |
|----|-----|---|-----|
| his | way | waits | |

4. Write **lay** and **laid** for these sentences.

   **a.** Kate _____ the quilt on the bed.

   **b.** Did Kate _____ it on the bed?

5. Spell two new words by adding **ing** to **lay** and **pay**. Circle the word that means "giving money for something."

Write the words for each picture. Draw a line under the words with the long **a** sound. Circle the snurks.

1.
a snail on a path
a snake on a path

2.
two pails of sand and rocks
two pails of gray paint

3.
four cakes on a tray
four plates of cake

4.
a gate that has been painted
a game that has been played

/ā/ stands for the long **a** sound in **play**, **train**, and **game**.

# Spelling Helps Reading

Sound out these Play Train Game words.

| | | | | | | |
|---|---|---|---|---|---|---|
| chase | cake | cane | cape | cave | clay | day |
| brain | gate | jail | jay | lake | made | maid |
| pain | plane | paint | plate | pray | rail | spade |
| snake | shade | rake | sail | tray | vase | sway |

Fit the right sentence parts together. Read the sentences.

1. To make a gray tray red,    I must have a spade.
2. To fix a gate,    I must have a rake.
3. To dig up some clay,    I must have paint.
4. To stack hay,    I may want a plate.
5. To bake a cake,    I may want nails.

6. To make a truck stop,    James trains his dog.
7. To raise a grain crop,    I step on the brake.
8. To wade in a lake,    I must have rain.
9. To make him shake hands,    Ray takes off his socks.
10. To stay safe from flames,    I do not play with matches.

Want to hold a Gray Paint Sale?
Want to send some Day Plane Mail?
You have three ways to spell that /ā/,
As in **train** and **game** and **play**.

# 7 We Keep Clean Words

| | | |
|---|---|---|
| street | free | team |
| teeth | sheep | least |
| sweet | dream | each |
| sweep | beat | ▽ dead |
| cheek | heat | ▽ bread |
| sheet | speak | |

The vowel sound in **We Keep Clean** words is called the long **e** sound.

**e** spells the long **e** sound in **we**.

**ee** spells the long **e** sound in **keep**.

**ea** spells the long **e** sound in **clean**.

**1.** Say the spelling words. Hear the vowel sounds.

34

**2.** Write the words in which **ee** spells the vowel sound. Draw a line under each **ee.**

**3.** Write the words in which **ea** spells the long **e** sound.

 Say **bread** and **dead.** Do you hear the long **e** sound? Why are **bread** and **dead** snurks?

**4.** Write **bread, dead,** and **great.** Draw a line under the words with the /e/ sound. Circle the word with the /ā/ sound.

**5.** Read the sentence. Write the words with the long **e** sound. Then write the snurks.

He wants his team to eat some bread.

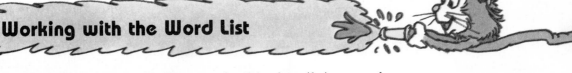

## Working with the Word List

**1.** Write the words that end with the /k/ sound.

**2.** Write the word for each picture.

 **a.**   **b.**    **c.**

*street* *cheek* *dream* *team*

*teeth* *sheet* *beat* *least*

*sweet* *free* *heat* *each*

*sweep* *sheep* *speak* *dead*

*bread*

**3.** Write the word for each picture.

a.  b. c.

**4.** Write the words with these meanings.

**a.** brush off   **b.** say   **c.** make hot

**d.** side of face   **e.** not held back   **f.** hit

**5.** Use the words to write what Jean said.

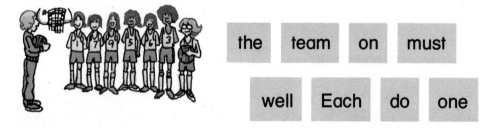

the   team   on   must

well   Each   do   one

**36**

# Building Spelling Power

**1.** Write new **ee** words.

   **a.** Change **sweep** to  .

   **b.** Change **seen** to  .

   **c.** Change **sweet** to  .

**2.** Write new **ea** words.

   **a.** Change **dream** to  .

   **b.** Change **each** to  .

**3.** Write a new **ea** word for each meaning.

   **a.** not strong     **b.** rich milk     **c.** yell

**4.** Write a new **ee** word for each meaning.

   **a.** take a nap     **b.** two plus one     **c.** 7 days

/ē/ stands for the long e sound in **we, keep,** and **clean.**

## Spelling Helps Reading

Sound out these We Keep Clean words.

| speech | beach | bee | cream | deep | east | feel |
|--------|-------|-----|-------|------|------|------|
| feed | green | keep | lead | lean | leap | meat |
| need | reach | read | sea | seed | seem | sleep |
| stream | queen | tea | teach | weak | wheel | mean |

For each row write two sets of words that go together.

| | | | | | | |
|----|-------|-------|--------|--------|--------|--------|
| 1. | three | green | two | gray | one | pink |
| 2. | beets | peas | peach | plum | grape | beans |
| 3. | clean | mean | cross | neat | sick | fresh |
| 4. | leap | creep | scream | jump | squeak | squeal |
| 5. | bee | sheep | flea | skunk | moth | fox |
| 6. | beef | cake | buns | bread | ham | veal |
| 7. | tree | grass | leaf | reeds | weeds | twig |
| 8. | creek | stream | lake | sleet | rain | hail |
| 9. | steel | spade | brass | tin | rake | brush |
| 10. | seed | bleed | peel | sheet | leash | leap |

You can spell an /ē/ with E
As in **we** and **she** and **me**,
With two E's (see **keep** and **sweet**)
Or with E-A (see **clean** and **neat**).

# 8 My Right Kind of Smile Words

| | | |
|---|---|---|
| sky | wind | pipe |
| fry | prize | smile |
| high | shine | drive |
| bright | slide | ripe ▽ child |
| grind | fire | wife ▽ wild |

The vowel sound in **My Right Kind of Smile** words is called the long **i** sound.

**y** spells the long **i** sound in **my**.

**igh** spells the long **i** sound in **right**.

**i** before **nd** spells the long **i** sound in **kind**.

**i**-consonant letter-**e** spells the long **i** sound in **smile**.

1. Say the spelling words. Hear the sounds.

2. Write the words with **i**-consonant letter-**e**.

sky     grind     slide     drive
fry     wind     fire     ripe
high     prize     pipe     wife
bright     shine     smile     child
wild

**3.** Write the words with **y** and with **igh.** Draw a line under each **y** and **igh.**

**4.** Write **kind** and the spelling words with **ind.**

Say **child** and **wild.**
Do we spell **child** and **wild** like the other long **i** words?
Why do we call **child** and **wild snurks?**

**5.** Write **child, trip, wild,** and **fix.** Draw a line under the words with the long **i** sound.

**6.** Write the word for each meaning.

    **a.** grin       **b.** gleaming       **c.** be bright

**40**

# Working with the Word List

**1.** Write a word for each of these starting sounds.

    **a.** /ch/       **b.** /sh/       **c.** /g/

    **d.** /f/        **e.** /f/        **f.** /b/

**2.** Write a word for each meaning.

    **a.** twist       **b.** not tame     **c.** slip

**3.** Use the words to write what she said.

| fire | bright | ! | light |
| --- | --- | --- | --- |

| This | a | makes |
| --- | --- | --- |

**4.** Use the words to write what the boy said.

| branches | are | high | on | The |
| --- | --- | --- | --- | --- |

| ripe | the | . | peaches |
| --- | --- | --- | --- |

## Building Spelling Power

**1.** Write the **i**-consonant letter-**e** word for each space.

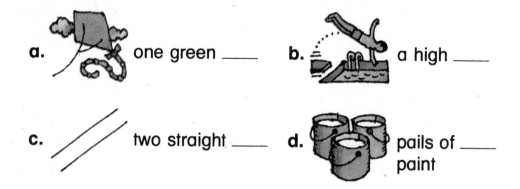

**a.** one green ____

**b.** a high ____

**c.** two straight ____

**d.** pails of ____ paint

**2.** Write the **igh** word for each space.

**a.** a bright ____

**b.** the ____ hand

**c.** the sky at ____

**d.** a prize ____

/ī/ stands for the long **i** sound in **my** and **right** and **kind** and **smile.**

Sound out these My Right Kind of Smile words.

| | | | | | | |
|---|---|---|---|---|---|---|
| sight | blind | cry | dime | dive | fight | find |
| quite | five | hide | fly | kind | light | strike |
| might | mile | mind | night | pile | wire | fright |
| rise | size | dry | spy | time | try | while |

Read the story. Answer the question at the end.

Jean and Mike needed kite string. The two stopped at a red light. A man with black glasses and a white cane was sitting on a bench with a tin cup in his hand.

"Jean," said Mike, "you will be helping me fly my kite. We must try to find that string."

"You can get fine kite string at Hine's Shop right in this block, my child," said the man. "The name is as big as life in bright green lights on the front."

The man smiled and wiped his glasses clean with a cloth. Mike and Jean got the string. On the way back Mike said, "I still have five dimes left. I might as well drop them in the blind man's cup."

"I think not," said Jean.

"Why not?" asked Mike. "You tell me to be kind."

Why did Jean not want Mike to be kind to the man?

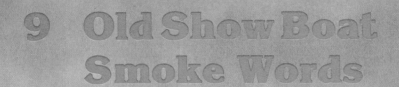

# 9 Old Show Boat Smoke Words

| | | | |
|---|---|---|---|
| sold | float | smoke | none |
| scold | soak | drove | most |
| throw | soak | spoke | |
| snow | load | broke | |
| grow | throat | rope | |

The vowel sound in **Old Show Boat Smoke** words is called the long **o** sound.

**o** before **ld** spells the long **o** sound in **old**.

**ow** spells the long **o** sound in **show**.

**oa** spells the long **o** sound in **boat**.

**o**-consonant letter-**e** spells the long **o** sound in **smoke**.

**1.** Say the spelling words. Write the words with **ow**.

44

**2.** Write the words with **oa.** Draw a line under the **oa** in each word.

**3.** Write the long **o** words that have **o**-consonant letter-**e.** Draw a line under each **o.** Circle each **e.**

**4.** Write the words with **old.** Draw a line under the **old** in each word.

Say **none** and **most.** Hear the two different vowel sounds.

Which word LOOKS like a long **o** word?

Which word SOUNDS like a long **o** word?

Why do we call **none** and **most** snurks?

**5.** Write **sure, most, front,** and **none.** Circle the words with the /u/ sound.

## Working with the Word List

**1.** Write the words with these meanings.

    **a.** not sink     **b.** toss     **c.** said

*sold grow load spoke*
*scold float throat broke*
*throw soak smoke rope*
*snow soap drove* ▽ *none*
▽ *most*

**2.** Write the spelling words. One is a snurk.

**a.** It cleans
things.

**b.** It comes
from fire.

**c.** It is cold
and wet.

**d.** It means
"not one."

**e.** We tie
with it.

**f.** It means
"fuss."

We say: "I make it. I made it.
We see it. We saw it.
We ride buses. We rode buses."

**3.** Write a spelling word for each space.

**a.** Did she **break** it?
Yes, she ____ it.

**b.** Did he ____ it?
Yes, he **grew** it.

**c.** Did he **drive** it?
Yes, he ____ it.

**d.** Did she **speak?**
Yes, she ____ .

# Building Spelling Power

**1.** Write the **old** word for each picture.

 a.  b.  c.

**2.** Write the two words in each box with the same vowel sound.

a.
| most |
| cost |
| cone |

b.
| goat |
| none |
| from |

c.
| snow |
| now |
| rope |

**3.** Each sentence has one spelling mistake and one other mistake. Write the sentences the right way.

 a.    This trick has a full load of coal

 b.    Joan sold five bag bowls

/ō/ stands for the long **o** sound in **old** and **show** and **boat**.

# Spelling Helps Reading

Sound out these words. Then read the story.

| those | bowl | blow | coach | coal | coat | woke |
| hold | gold | goat | goal | fold | cone | cold |
| hole | hope | joke | hose | nose | old | bold |
| toast | told | stove | stone | shone | slow | pole |

Miss Jones's class had been telling jokes.

"My dad told me an old one," said Rose Sloan. "It is not a joke, but a kind of trick. On the road home, a man has to cross a stream. He has a mean dog, a goat, and a sack of oats. The man's boat can hold just him and his dog in one load. It can hold him and his goat. It can hold him and the oats."

Kate Stokes spoke up. "You mean he must row the boat to and fro to get one at a time?"

"Yes, Kate. But if the dog is left with the goat, he will have him by the throat in no time. The dog will not eat the oats, but the goat will. The dog may not be left with the goat, but he can be left with the oats. The goat cannot be left with the dog or with the oats. So the trick is to get those three home."

**Can you show Rose the way to do it?**

48

# 10 Make-Making Words

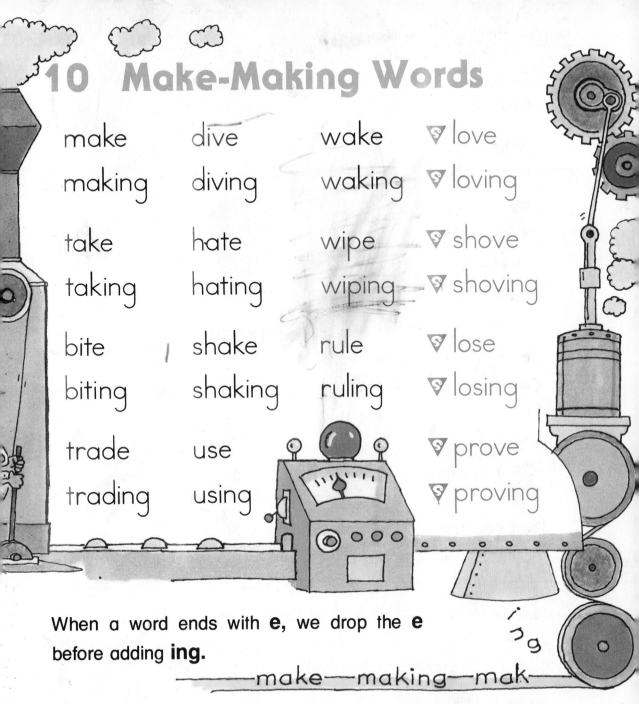

| | | | |
|---|---|---|---|
| make | dive | wake | love |
| making | diving | waking | loving |
| take | hate | wipe | shove |
| taking | hating | wiping | shoving |
| bite | shake | rule | lose |
| biting | shaking | ruling | losing |
| trade | use | | prove |
| trading | using | | proving |

When a word ends with **e,** we drop the **e** before adding **ing.**

make—making—mak

**1.** Say the spelling words. Write the /ā/ words spelled **a**-consonant letter-**e.** Then write each word with its **ing** ending.

**49**

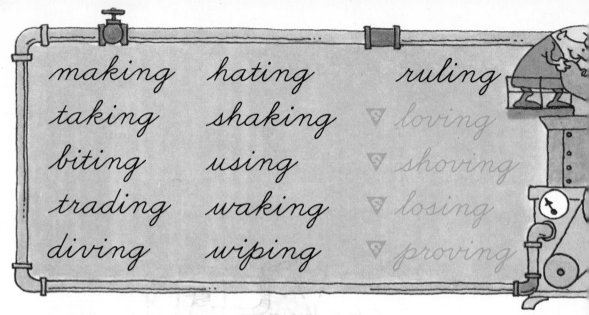

*making   hating   ruling*
*taking   shaking   loving*
*biting   using   shoving*
*trading   waking   losing*
*diving   wiping   proving*

**2.** Write the /ī/ words spelled **i**-consonant letter-**e**. Then write each word with its **ing** ending.

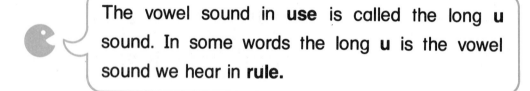

The vowel sound in **use** is called the long **u** sound. In some words the long **u** is the vowel sound we hear in **rule.**

**3.** Write the words with **u**-consonant letter-**e**. Then write each word with its **ing** ending.

Say the snurks. Hear the vowel sounds.
Which vowel sound do you hear in **love** and **shove?** Which vowel sound do you hear in **lose** and **prove?**
Which vowel sound does **o**-consonant letter-**e** spell in most words?

**50**

**4.** Write the **ing** snurk for each picture.

a.   b.   c.

## Working with the Word List

**1.** Write the opposites. The words are in the word list.

    **a.** finding        **b.** loving        **c.** giving

    **d.** hating        **e.** sleeping    **f.** saving

**2.** Each sentence has one misspelled word and one other mistake. Write the sentences the right way.

**a.**     she is taking a big bit.

**b.**     Don and mike are shakeing this tree.

51

## Building Spelling Power

**1.** Some words do not change when we add **ing.**

      ask—asking   eat—eating   go—going

Write the **ing** words for these pictures.

**a.**                **b.**                **c.**

**2.** When a word ends with one vowel letter and one consonant, we double the last consonant before adding **ing.**

      hit—hitting   run—running

Write the **ing** words for these pictures.

**a.**                **b.**                **c.**

**3.** When a word ends with **e,** we drop the **e** before **ing.**

      like—liking   shine—shining

Write the **ing** words for these pictures.

**a.**                **b.**                **c.**

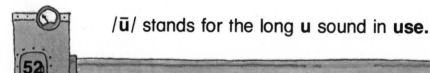

/ū/ stands for the long **u** sound in **use.**

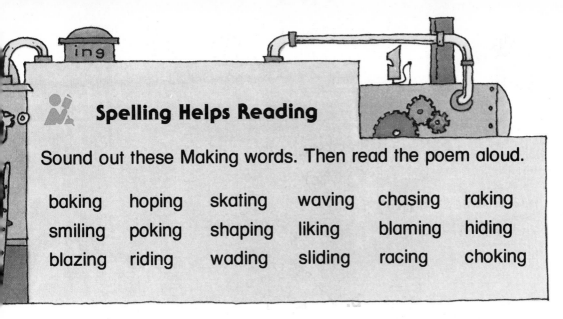

## Spelling Helps Reading

Sound out these Making words. Then read the poem aloud.

| | | | | | |
|---|---|---|---|---|---|
| baking | hoping | skating | waving | chasing | raking |
| smiling | poking | shaping | liking | blaming | hiding |
| blazing | riding | wading | sliding | racing | choking |

Drop the **e** and add the **ing**

And you'll make the **ing** verbs sing.

Fish are biting, bakers baking,

Divers diving, shakers shaking,

Skaters skating, waders wading,

Voters voting, traders trading,

Smilers smiling, wipers wiping,

Users using, gripers griping,

Hopers hoping, rakers raking,

Flags are waving, makers making,

Cowboys roping, sleepers waking,

Filers filing, takers taking,

Pipers piping, racers racing,

Snipers sniping, chasers chasing!

Same old rule. It always works,

Even with those snurky snurks!

# 11 Large Judge Words

| | | | | |
|---|---|---|---|---|
| jug | age | page | change | edge |
| joke | cage | huge | large | bridge |
| jail | rage | strange | charge | judge |

We use both **g** and **j** to spell words that start with the  sound: **judge, gym.**

We use **ge** and **dge** to spell the  sound at the end of words.

**ge** spells the  sound after consonant letters and after long-vowel sounds: **large, huge.**

**dge** spells the  sound after short-vowel sounds: **judge, edge.**

**1.** Write the four words that start with the  sound.

54

**2.** Write the **dge** words. Draw a line under the letters that spell the short-vowel sounds.

**3.** Write the words in which **ge** spells the  sound. Circle the words in which **ge** follows a long-vowel letter.

> Say **large** and **charge.** Hear the vowel and /r/ sounds. The sounds that start  are spelled **ar.**

**4.** Write the words in which **ge** follows a consonant letter. Circle the words that have the sounds that start  .

**5.** Write the words that mean "big." Circle the word with /ū/.

**6.** Write **change** and **charge** with **ing** endings.

**a.** She is ＿＿ the tire.　**b.** He is ＿＿ a dime.

**7.** Write each sentence. Then write **true** or **false.**

**a.** This page has just one edge.

**b.** Fine jokes should make us smile at least.

jug   cage   strange   edge
joke   rage   change   bridge
jail   page   large   judge
age   huge   charge

## Working with the Word List

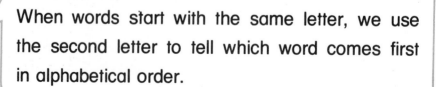

These words are in **alphabetical order:**

     jail    joke    jug

When words start with the same letter, we use the second letter to tell which word comes first in alphabetical order.

**1.** Write the **dge** words in alphabetical order.

**2.** Write the seven /ā/ words in alphabetical order.

**3.** Write the word for each meaning.

   **a.** odd       **b.** switch      **c.** rim

# Building Spelling Power

**1.** Change the starting letters to spell new words.

  **a.** Change **page** to  .

  **b.** Change **keep** to  .

  **c.** Change **let** to  .

  **d.** Change **judge** to  .

**2.** Write the two questions. Use question marks.

  **a.**

| have | fudge | ? | I |

| May | pieces | of | two |

  **b.**

| on | What | the | stage |

| Jack | is | ? | doing |

 /j/ stands for the  sound in **judge.**

57

## Spelling Helps Reading

Sound out these Large Judge words. Then read the story.

| badge | fudge | jam | job | ledge | range |
|-------|-------|-------|------|-------|--------|
| barge | grudge | jeans | jump | jog | trudge |
| budge | hedge | jet | just | jeep | ridge |
| dodge | hinge | jab | junk | stage | lodge |

Jack and Madge Page's dad had just changed jobs. The new job was on a barge and it paid high wages. He was in charge of a huge crane that dredged up mud and sludge from the bed of a deep stream.

One day he left his lunch box at home.

"Jack," said Mrs. Page, "take dad's lunch to him. Madge, put on those jeans and go with Jack."

Jack and Madge trudged off to the edge of the stream.

"I see Dad!" cried Madge. "His barge is right at that low bridge that crosses the stream."

"That barge is a long way off," said Jack. "We have no boat. Dad has no boat. His boss will not bring the barge in. I cannot throw the box from the bank."

"Come on, Jack," cried Madge. "I will show you the way to get the lunch box to Dad."

Can you tell the way Madge did it?

# 12 Nice Place Words

| | | | | |
|---|---|---|---|---|
| ice | mice | race | space | fence |
| nice | rice | face | dance | since |
| twice | slice | place | chance | voice |

 once

We use both **s** and **c** to spell words that start with the ☀ sound: **sent, cent.**

We use **s** and **ss** and **ce** to spell words that end with the ☀ sound: **bus, glass, nice, place.**

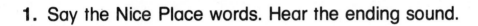

**1.** Say the Nice Place words. Hear the ending sound.

**2.** Write the words with the /ī/ sound. Circle each **ce**.

**3.** Write the four words with the /ā/ sound. Circle each **ce**.

ice    rice    place    fence
nice   slice   space    since
twice  race    dance    voice
mice   face    chance   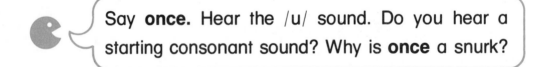once

Say **voice.** Hear the vowel sound.
We use **oi** to spell the vowel sound in **voice.**
We use **oy** to spell the vowel sound in **boy.**

**4.** Write **voice, dance, chance, fence,** and **since.** Draw a line under the words with the /a/ sound.

Say **once.** Hear the /u/ sound. Do you hear a starting consonant sound? Why is **once** a snurk?

**5.** Write **once, fence, sure,** and **front.** Draw a line under each snurk.

**6.** Write the words in which **s** spells the ☀ sound.

**60**

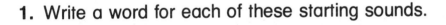

## Working with the Word List

**1.** Write a word for each of these starting sounds.

    **a.** /s/           **b.** /s/           **c.** /s/

    **d.** /ch/         **e.** /ī/           **f.** /d/

    **g.** /f/           **h.** /f/           **i.** /v/

    **j.** /r/           **k.** /r/          **l.** /m/

**2.** Each sentence has one mistake. Write the sentences right.

    **a.**                  It would be nice to win the rice.

    **b.**                  The mice got in a fine save place.

    **c.** A dish of hat steaming rice tastes nice.

    **d. Twice** means "three times."

## Building Spelling Power

**1.** The words **dance, race,** and **slice** can be used as verbs. Write the three words with their **ing** endings.

**2.** The words **voice, chance,** and **face** can be used as nouns. Write the three words with the **s** ending to show "more than one."

**3.** Write **rice.** Change **r** to **pr** and to **sp** and write two new words. Circle the word that means "cost."

**4.** Write **since.** Change **s** to **m** and to **pr** and write two new words. Circle the word that means "chop up."

**5.** Write **voice.** Change **v** to **ch** and write a new word. Circle the word that means "the one you want most."

**6.** Write these sentences. Use words you wrote for this page to fill the spaces.

    **a.** What you pay is the _____ of a thing.

    **b.** A _____ is the child of a king.

    **c.** We add _____ to make food taste nice.

      /oi/ stands for the vowel sound in **boy.**
      /oi/ stands for the vowel sound in **voice.**

## Spelling Helps Reading

Sound out these words. Then read the story.

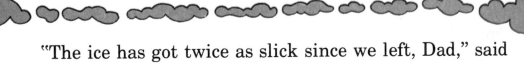

| | | | | | | |
|---|---|---|---|---|---|---|
| brace | choice | dice | juice | lace | peace | price |
| prince | spice | trace | mince | prance | lice | splice |
| pace | grace | dunce | fleece | glance | lance | ace |

"The ice has got twice as slick since we left, Dad," said Bruce. "Do we have a chance to get home?"

"Face it, Bruce," said Mr. Vance. "This old truck could not win a race, but...." BANG!

Mr. Vance groaned. "A flat!" he cried. "And right on the old bridge! Lace up that nice fleece-lined coat, Bruce, and give me a hand at once."

He jacked up the truck and twisted off the five lugs that held the wheel. He placed them in the hubcap on the fence rail. Bruce stamped his feet to stay warm.

"O.K.," cried Mr. Vance, his voice shaking from the cold. "Hand me the lugs, Bruce."

But just then the wind sent the hubcap flying. The five lugs sank in the stream.

"Dad, we need at least three lugs to hold the wheel on tight," cried Bruce. "Why not..."

Can you tell what Bruce is going to say?

# 13 Twelve Geese Words

| | | | | |
|---|---|---|---|---|
| else | leave | geese | solve | ☞ paste |
| tease | sense | sneeze | sleeve | ☞ taste |
| raise | noise | twelve | please | ☞ waste |

**Twelve Geese** words have an extra silent **e** at the end.

1. Say the words in the spelling list. Hear the sounds.

2. Write the four short-vowel words. Draw a line under each silent **e.**

3. Write the words in which two vowel letters together spell a long-vowel sound. Draw a line under the words with the /ē/ sound.

Say **waste, taste,** and **paste.** Hear the vowel sound. Which letter spells the /ā/ sound in each word? Why do we call the words snurks?

**4.** Write the four words with the /ā/ sound. Draw a line under each of the snurks.

**5.** Write **noise, raise,** and **please.** Draw a line under the word with the /oi/ sound.

**6.** Write the five words that end with the /z/ sound. Circle the word in which **z** spells /z/.

# Working with the Word List

**1.** Write the word for each picture. Draw a line under the noun that names "more than one."

**a.**

**b.**

**c.**

**2.** Write the word for each meaning.

   **a.** lift       **b.** ten plus two    **c.** go

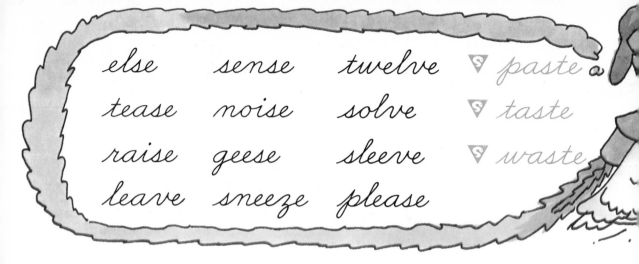

*else*    *sense*    *twelve*    *paste*

*tease*    *noise*    *solve*    *taste*

*raise*    *geese*    *sleeve*    *waste*

*leave*    *sneeze*    *please*

**3.** Write the word for each meaning. Two words are snurks.

   **a.** make bad use of    **b.** eat just a bit    **c.** play tricks on

**4.** Use five of these words to fill the spaces in the sentences:
**else, solve, please, sense, since, noise, paste, was.**

   **a.**          Do not make so much ____, ____.

   **b.**          I can ____ it. Who ____ can do it?

   **c.**          This dog has a fine ____ of smell.

**66**

# Building Spelling Power

 We do not always add **s** or **es** to words to spell "more than one." Sometimes we write new words with new vowel sounds. We write **man** for "one" and **men** for "more than one."

**1.** Write the "more than one" word for each picture.

a.　　　　　　　b.　　　　　　　c.

**2.** Write **leaves, elves,** and **loaves.** Circle the word with the /ē/ sound.

**3.** Write two words from Exercise 2 to fill the spaces.

 These ＿＿ have three huge ＿＿ of bread.

/t/ stands for the sound that starts **tease** and **twelve.**

/p/ stands for the sound that starts **paste** and **please.**

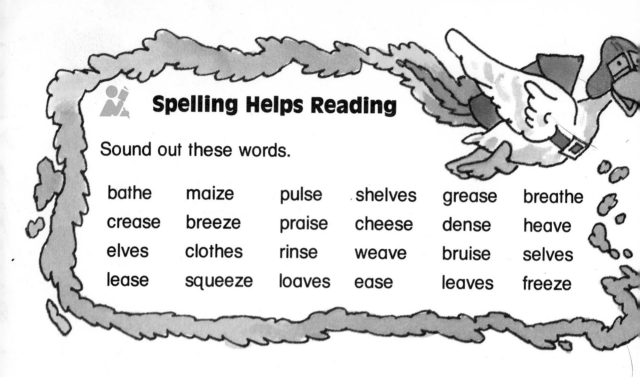

# Spelling Helps Reading

Sound out these words.

| | | | | | |
|---|---|---|---|---|---|
| bathe | maize | pulse | shelves | grease | breathe |
| crease | breeze | praise | cheese | dense | heave |
| elves | clothes | rinse | weave | bruise | selves |
| lease | squeeze | loaves | ease | leaves | freeze |

Read the sentences. Write **T (true)** or **F (false)** for each sentence.

1. Five coats are sure to have at least twelve sleeves.
2. Wild geese like to fly east when it gets cold.
3. Mice love the taste of a piece of cheese.
4. Those who want to make peace should be praised.
5. You could freeze a lot of grape juice with one ice cube.
6. If you sneeze once, you can be sure you have a cold.
7. If you have a long nose, you must have a keen sense of smell.
8. You can rinse soiled clothes in a tub.
9. Boys with soft voices make a lot of noise when they speak.
10. It is a waste of time to paste stamps on mail.

# 14 Cool Wool Words

1. boot
2. cool
3. tooth
4. pool
noon
broom

roof
shoot
5. truth
hook
brook
poor

shook
stood
wool
cook

We use **oo** to spell the sounds in **Cool Wool** words.

**oo** spells the vowel sound in  and in **cool**.

**oo** spells the vowel sound in  and in **wool**.

**1.** Write the **oo** words with the vowel sound in  .

**2.** Write the **oo** words with the vowel sound in  .

boot    noon    truth    shook

cool    broom    hook    stood

tooth    roof    brook    wool

pool    shoot    poor    cook

Say **truth.** Hear the vowel sound.
Does **truth** sound like a Cool word?
Does **truth** have an **oo** spelling?
Why do we call **truth** a snurk?

**3.** Write **truth, too, took,** and **tooth.** Draw a line under the words with the same vowel sound.

## Working with the Word List

**1.** Write ,  , and  in alphabetical order.

Circle the word that starts with the /t/ sound.

**2.** Write ,  , and  in alphabetical order.

Circle the word that starts and ends with the /k/ sound.

**70**

**3.** Write the word for each meaning.

**a.** fleece from sheep    **b.** a stream    **c.** not hot, not cold

**d.** midday    **e.** top of house    **f.** kind of shoe

We say: "I give it. I gave it.

He breaks it. He broke it.

You are good. You were good."

**4.** Use spelling words to fill the spaces.

**a.**

Did they **stand** up?

Yes, they ＿＿ up.

**b.**

Did she **shake** it?

Yes, she ＿＿ it.

**c.**

He did not tell a lie.

He told the ＿＿.

**d.**

Did I ＿＿ straight?

Yes, you **shot** straight.

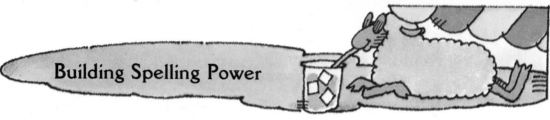

# Building Spelling Power

**1.** Say the Cool Wool picture words. Write the words.

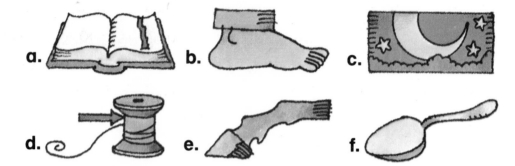

a.

b.

c.

d.

e.

f.

**2.** Each sentence has one spelling mistake and one other mistake. Write the sentences the right way.

a. The crook is chasing the poor goose?

b. The book is too Big.

c. she is sitting on a stood.

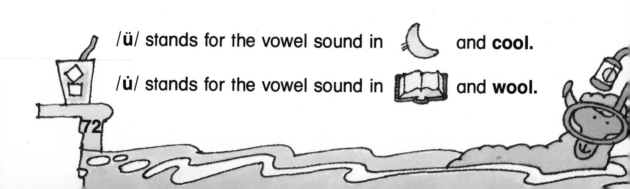

/ü/ stands for the vowel sound in 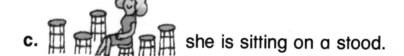 and **cool.**

/u̇/ stands for the vowel sound in and **wool.**

72

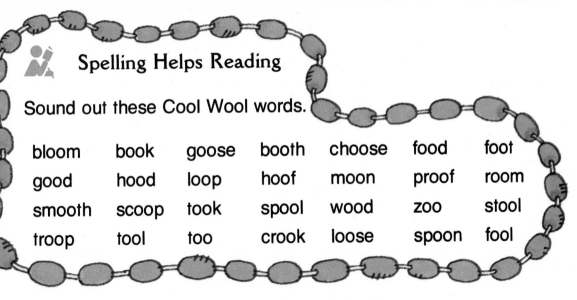

## Spelling Helps Reading

Sound out these Cool Wool words.

| | | | | | | |
|---|---|---|---|---|---|---|
| bloom | book | goose | booth | choose | food | foot |
| good | hood | loop | hoof | moon | proof | room |
| smooth | scoop | took | spool | wood | zoo | stool |
| troop | tool | too | crook | loose | spoon | fool |

Be ready to read the poem aloud to your class.

## LOOK!

I see nice words like **pool** and **tool**
And **fool** and **stool** and **school** and **spool**,
But find I have no spelling ~~rool~~ rule.

Then I see **boot** and **shoot** and **tooth**,
But meet a pretty girl named ~~Rooth~~ Ruth.

I see **noon** and **spoon** and **moon**,
But pretty **soon** I find it's ~~Joon~~ June.

I see **loop** and **stoop** and **droop**,
But have to **scoop** flies from my ~~soop~~ soup.

I see **cook** and **book** and **shook**
And **crook** and **brook** and **look** and **took**,
But when I **goof,** I am a ~~schnuck~~ schnook!

73

# 15 Maud's Small Shawl Words

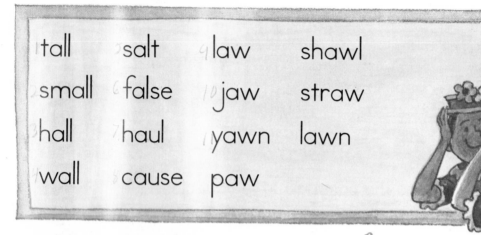

| tall | salt | law | shawl |
| small | false | jaw | straw |
| hall | haul | yawn | lawn |
| wall | cause | paw | |

**Maud's Small Shawl** words have the  vowel sound.

**au** spells the vowel sound in **Maud.**

**a** before **l** spells the vowel sound in **small.**

**aw** spells the vowel sound in **shawl.**

**1.** Say the spelling words. Hear the vowel sounds.

**2.** Write the two **au** words. Draw a line under the word with an extra silent **e** at the end.

**3.** Write the six words with **a** before **l.** Draw a line under the words that do not have a doubled consonant.

**74**

**4.** Write the seven **aw** words. Draw a line under the words that do not end with the vowel sound.

**5.** Write the word for each picture. Draw a line under the word with a two-letter consonant sound.

 **a.**    **b.**    **c.**

## Working with the Word List

**1.** Write the verb for the picture. Then write it with **s, ed,** and **ing** endings.

**2.** Write the word for each meaning. Circle the word that starts with the /t/ sound.

   **a.** high      **b.** not true      **c.** dried stems
                                            of grain

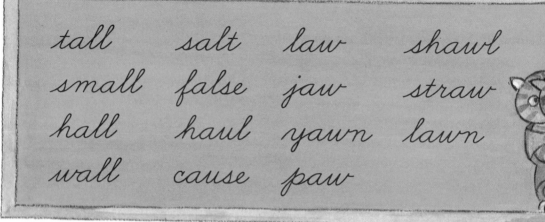

**3.** Write the word for each meaning.

    **a.** drag       **b.** a rule       **c.** not large

We write: "Maud's shawl. The cat's paw." We use an **apostrophe** and **s** to show that Maud owns the shawl. The cat owns the paw.

**4.** Use the words to write a sentence. Use a period.

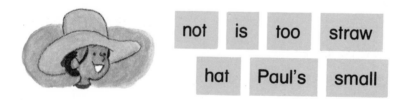

not   is   too   straw

hat   Paul's   small

**5.** Use the words to write a sentence. Use a question mark.

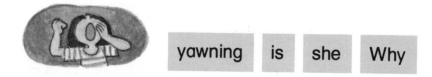

yawning   is   she   Why

# Building Spelling Power

**1.** Change the starting letters to write new words.

   **a.** Change **law** to  .

   **b.** Change **law** to  .

   **c.** Change **yawn** to  .

   **d.** Change **salt** to  .

   **e.** Change **shawl** to  .

   **f.** Change **tall** to  .

**2.** Use four of these words for the missing words in the sentence: **salt, balls, straw, saws, shoes, malt.** Write the sentence. Use commas between the words.

He buys ____, ____, ____, and ____.

/ô/ stands for the vowel sound in **Maud, small,** and **shawl.**

77

## Spelling Helps Reading

Sound out these words. Then read the story.

| | | | | | | |
|---|---|---|---|---|---|---|
| bald | call | caw | claw | fawn | dawn | drawn |
| fault | haunt | hawk | sauce | saw | stall | malt |
| halt | pause | raw | crawl | squawk | thaw | fall |

"Caw! Caw! Caw!"

"What is that, Aunt Maud?" called Paul.

"That is just Jim, the crow," said Paul's aunt. "I leave a loaf of stale bread on the front lawn. At dawn Jim scratches and claws it to pieces. He must be squawking at Flag. He thinks he should have all of it."

"Flag? Who—or what—is Flag?" asked Paul.

Just then he caught sight of a small tan thing with long, thin legs come trotting from the woods.

"That is Flag," said Aunt Maud. "She is quite tame. In fact, I taught Flag to lick salt from my hand. She has such big, sad eyes and soft, tan skin with white spots, as you can see. She will pause to eat what bread Jim left. Then she may take a nap in that straw pile. So, Paul, when you get back home, you can tell Mom and Dad that you saw a . . . ."

What was the thing that Paul saw?

78

# 16 Loud Crowd Words

| crowd | clown | proud |
|-------|-------|-------|
| town | mouse | shout |
| drown | loud | cloud |
| growl | ground | mouth |
| frown | round | count |

**Loud Crowd** words have the vowel sound that starts .

**ou** spells the vowel sound in **loud**.

**ow** spells the vowel sound in **crowd**.

**1.** Write the words with **ou**. Circle the word with silent **e** at the end.

crowd frown ground cloud
town clown round mouth
drown mouse proud count
growl loud shout

**2.** Write the words with **ow.** Circle the words that start with the /k/ sound.

**3.** Write a word for each of these starting sounds.

    **a.** /t/         **b.** /sh/         **c.** /l/

    **d.** /d/         **e.** /g/         **f.** /g/

**4.** Write the word for each meaning.

    **a.** call out         **b.** scowl         **c.** in the shape
                                                     of a ball

## Working with the Word List

**1.** Change one word in the sentence to make the sentence fit the picture. Write the sentence the right way.

    Why does that clown smile?

**2.** Change one word in the sentence to make it fit the picture. Write the sentence the right way.

What has that owl done?

**3.** Write the word for each of these meanings.

**a.** soil; a piece of land    **b.** filled with pride    **c.** not soft

> To put words in alphabetical order when the first two letters are the same, use the third letter: **ouch, out, owl.**
>
> To put words in alphabetical order when the first three letters are the same, use the fourth letter: **cloud, clown, crowd.**

**4.** Write the words for the pictures in alphabetical order.

**5.** Write **town, loud,** and **mouse** in alphabetical order. Circle the words that may be used as nouns, or "naming words."

## Building Spelling Power

We use **ow** to spell the vowel sound in **owl**. We use **ow** to spell the /ō/ sound, too: **blow, grow, show, own.**

**1.** Write these **ow** words with the /ō/ sound.

a.             b.             c.

**2.** Write the picture words. Use the printed words to help you. Circle the one /ō/ word you write.

 clown    b.  growl    c.  now

a.

 count    e.  grow    f.  round

d.

/**ou**/ stands for the vowel sound in **loud** and **crowd.**

82

## Spelling Helps Reading

Sound out these words. Then read the story.

| | | | | | | |
|---|---|---|---|---|---|---|
| brown | couch | bound | now | out | plow | howl |
| down | cow | grouch | how | bounce | scout | sound |
| house | flour | pouch | mouse | owl | pound | pout |
| our | blouse | noun | ouch | spout | hound | trout |

"I am thinking of a thing with an /ou/ sound," said Jane. "It breathes, so it is not a house, a cloud, a couch, a gown—not a thing like that."

"Does it hoot? Does it give milk?" asked Jack.

"No, it is not an owl and not a cow."

"Does it like cheese? Do cats pounce on it?" asked Ann. "Does it have a snout? Is it stout?"

"No, it is not a mouse and it is not a sow."

"I have it!" shouted Paul. "It makes a growling sound."

"No, it is not a hound, Paul."

"Does it swim?" asked Mike. "Is it good to eat?"

"It is not a trout, Mike."

"We are stumped," said Marge. "Give us a hint."

"Well," said Jane, "it comes to town once in a while. It is funny. It paints its face."

**What is it?**

# 17 Tough Group Snurks

▽ ought     ▽ fourth     ▽ through

▽ bought     ▽ course     ▽ though

▽ fought     ▽ pour     ▽ touch

▽ brought     ▽ group     ▽ rough

▽ thought     ▽ soup     ▽ tough

**Tough Group** snurks are words in which **ou** does not spell the /ou/ vowel sound we hear in **loud**.

**Tough Group** snurks have these vowel sounds:

> /u/ as in **up**     /ô/ as in **off**
>
> /ü/ as in **two**     /ō/ as in **old**

**1.** Write the three Tough Group words with the /u/ sound.

**2.** Write the Tough Group words with the /ü/ sound.

**3.** Write **four** and the Tough Group words with the same /ôr/ sounds as **four**.

**4.** Write the **ough** words with the /ô/ sound.

**5.** Write **slow, smoke,** and the Tough Group word with the same /ō/ sound as **slow** and **smoke.**

## Working with the Word List

> **gh** spells the /f/ sound in two spelling words.
> **gh** is silent in seven spelling words.
> Say all the spelling words that have **gh.**

**1.** Write the words in which **gh** spells the /f/ sound. Circle the word that means "not smooth."

**2.** Write the words with silent **gh.**

**3.** Write the sentence in the box. Underline the two words with the /ô/ sound. Circle the word with the /ü/ sound.

> We bought four cans of soup and brought them home.

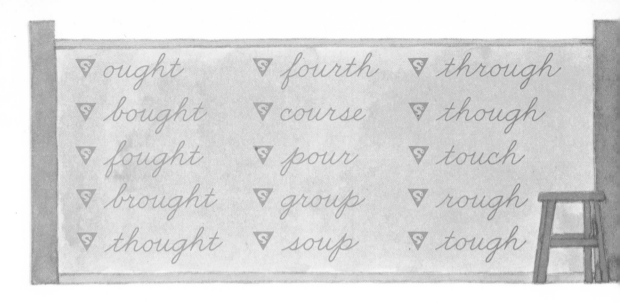

ought     fourth     through
bought     course     though
fought     pour     touch
brought     group     rough
thought     soup     tough

**4.** Use words from the spelling list to fill the spaces. Write the words.

**a.**  She will ____ ____ in the ____ bowl.

**b.**  The young man is rowing ____ ____ waves.

**c.**  Of ____ you should not ____ a hot stove.

**d.**  They like the meat ____ it is ____.

**e.**  That ____ of girls ____ the basketball.

# Building Spelling Power

 We say: "I do it now. I did it then.

I see it now. I saw it then."

**1.** Write the missing words.

a. Did she **buy** it?

Yes, she _____ it.

b. Did they **fight?**

Yes, they _____.

c. Did he **bring** your mail?

Yes, he _____ it.

d. Did you **think** you would win?

Yes, I _____ I would win.

**2.** Two words have the wrong spellings. Write the two words the right way.

a.  tuch    b.  soop    c. boot

/r/ stands for the sound that starts **rough.**

## Spelling Helps Reading

Say these Tough Group snurks.

| | | | | |
|---|---|---|---|---|
| thought | rough | four | you | course |
| bought | tough | fourth | your | young |
| fought | group | though | pour | touch |
| brought | soup | dough | tour | through |

Follow along as your teacher reads the poem aloud. Then read the poem aloud with your classmates.

I have been thinking all this week,
We **ought** to spell the way we speak.
If we can say those sounds like **awt,**
Why must we spell them **bought** and **brought?**
And also **fought?** (That's what I **thought!**)
If we say **groop,** why spell it **group?**
And then there's **soop.** Why spell it **soup?**
Why do they let us roll a **hoop?**
Or make our wilted flowers **droop?**
And then we have both **through** and **though,**
And **touch** and **pour** and **course** and **dough.**
I say they make it mighty **tough.**
It's time to stop, I've had **enough!**
Oh, they do sneak and they do lurk!
I've had it with this **ou** snurk.

88

| | | |
|---|---|---|
| dirt | verse | purse |
| shirt | jerk | ᔕ earn |
| skirt | burn | ᔕ learn |
| whirl | church | ᔕ search |
| perch | nurse | ᔕ earth |

All **Turn the Bird Perch** words have the same vowel-r sounds.

**ur** spells the vowel-r sounds in **turn**.
**ir** spells the vowel-r sounds in **bird**.
**er** spells the vowel-r sounds in **perch**.

**ear** spells the vowel-r sounds in the snurks **earn, learn, search,** and **earth.**

**1.** Say the **er** words. Write them.

| | | | |
|---|---|---|---|
| dirt | perch | burn | ⬇ earn |
| shirt | verse | church | ⬇ learn |
| skirt | jerk | nurse | ⬇ search |
| whirl | | purse | ⬇ earth |

**2.** Say the **ir** words. Write them.

**3.** Say the **ur** words. Write them.

Say the four snurks.

Do they sound like Turn the Bird Perch words?

Why do we call **earn, learn, search,** and **earth** snurks?

**4.** Write the **ear** snurks. Circle the word that means "try to find by looking through."

## Working with the Word List

**1.** Write the words that start with these two-letter consonant sounds. Circle the word that means "spin fast."

    **a.** /ch/         **b.** /hw/         **c.** /sh/

**2.** Write the words that end with these consonant sounds. Circle the word you write that means "a place where a bird may sit."

**a.** /ch/ **b.** /ch/ **c.** /ch/

**d.** /k/ **e.** /th/ **f.** /l/

**3.** Write 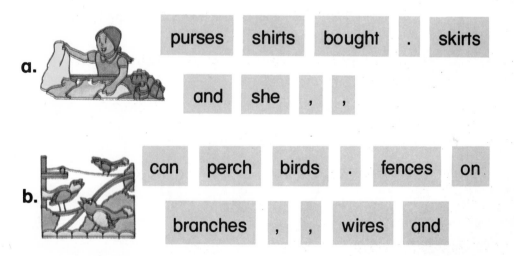 , , and another spelling word that rhymes with these words.

**4.** Use the words to write sentences. Remember to use commas between the words in a list of things.

**a.**

| purses | shirts | bought | . | skirts |

| and | she | , | , |

**b.**

| can | perch | birds | . | fences | on |

| branches | , | , | wires | and |

**5.** Write the word that means "to be on fire." Then write the word with **ed** and with **ing.**

**6.** Write the word that means "to try to find by looking." Then write the word with **ed** and with **ing.**

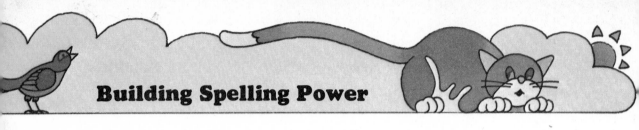

## Building Spelling Power

 We can add **er** to words to spell new words.
We write **rich—richer, poor—poorer.**

**1.** Add **er** to each of these six words. Write the new **er** word for each **er** word with the opposite meaning below.

kind     small     loud     slow     high     young

**a.** softer      **b.** faster      **c.** older

**d.** lower      **e.** greater      **f.** meaner

**2.** Write Fern's question and the clerk's answer.

**a.** "_____?" asked Fern.      **b.** "_____," said the clerk.

the    girls'    purses

Where    are

on    Right    shelf

there    the    third

/ėr/ stands for the vowel-r sounds in **turn, bird,** and **perch.**

## Spelling Helps Reading

Sound out these Turn the Bird Perch words.

| | | | | | | |
|---|---|---|---|---|---|---|
| turn | germ | verb | clerk | firm | stir | third |
| chirp | snurk | bird | fern | first | girl | thirst |
| burp | curl | burst | curve | serve | sir | hurt |

Read the story. Answer the question.

Mr. Burke had bought a large boat. He and his daughter Bert were showing it to a group of boys and girls in Bert's third grade class.

"I had to learn some boating terms," said Bert. "The back end of the boat is the stern. Beds are called berths. Those birds perched on the sails are terns. Rough waves bursting in on the sand are surf. The sea rises and falls. We call that the tides."

"Let us see how clever you kids are," said Mr. Burke. "See that rope ladder hanging from the side of the boat? The tide rises one foot each hour. Each rung on the ladder is one foot from the next one. The tide is touching the fourth rung now at noon. When will the tide rise to the first rung?"

"At three o'clock, of course, sir," cried Herb.

Was Herb right?

# 19 More Corn Starch Words

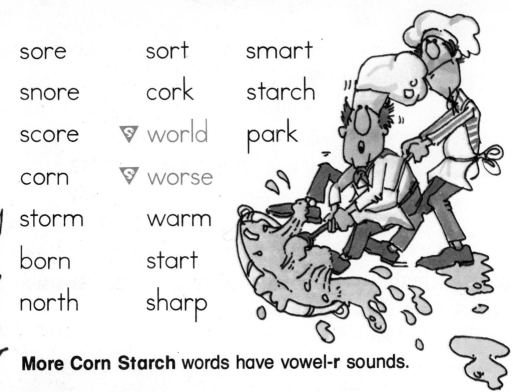

| sore | sort | smart |
|------|------|-------|
| snore | cork | starch |
| score | ⚡ world | park |
| corn | ⚡ worse | |
| storm | warm | |
| born | start | |
| north | sharp | |

**More Corn Starch** words have vowel-**r** sounds.

**More Corn** words have the vowel-**r** sounds you hear in  .

The sounds are spelled **ore** and **or.**

**Starch** words have the vowel-**r** sounds that start  .

The sounds are spelled **ar.**

**1. Say the six ar words. Write them.**

**2.** Say the three **ore** words. Write them.

**3.** Say the six **or** words. Write them. Circle the word that means "brought to life."

> Say **world** and **worse.** Hear the sounds.
> What vowel-**r** sounds do you hear in **world?**
> What vowel-**r** sounds do you hear in **worse?**
> Why do we call these two words snurks?

**4.** Write **world, worse, more,** and **church.** Circle the words that have the same vowel-**r** sounds.

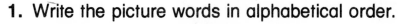

## Working with the Word List

**1.** Write the picture words in alphabetical order.

**2.** Write the words that start with these sounds.

    **a.** /k/         **b.** /k/         **c.** /sh/

    **d.** /w/         **e.** /w/         **f.** /w/

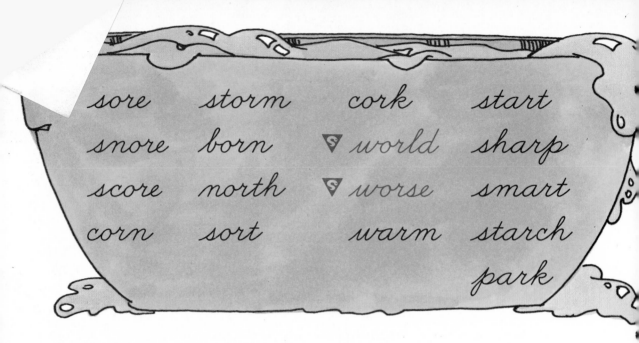

sore    storm    cork    start

snore    born    world    sharp

score    north    worse    smart

corn    sort    warm    starch

park

**3.** Write words that are the opposites of these words.

    **a.** dull        **b.** south        **c.** cool

**4.** Each sentence has one word that is not spelled right. Write the word the right way.

    **a.** The pin has a sharp paint.

    **b.** Jugs need smell corks.

    **c.** Mark was barn on June 25.

    **d.** The word **work** start with **w.**

**5.** Write the spelling word for each meaning.

    **a.** painful place    **b.** less well,    **c.** make a point
        on the skin        more ill         in a game

# Building Spelling Power

**1.** Write **sort.** Then change **s** to **p** and to **f** to write new words. Circle the word you write that means "a place for ships to come."

**2.** Write **cork.** Then change **c** to **p** and to **f** to write new words. Circle the word that means "an eating tool."

**3.** Write **park.** Then change **p** to **m** and to **d** to write new words. Circle the word that means "with no light."

**4.** Write **warm.** Then change **w** to **h** and to **f** to write new words. Circle the word that means "hurt."

**5.** Say the twelve words you wrote in this lesson. Write the four nouns that name places.

**6.** Say **pork, mark, farm,** and **dark.** Write the two words that rhyme.

/ôr/ stands for the vowel-**r** sounds in **more** and **corn.**
/är/ stands for the vowel-**r** sounds in **starch.**

## Spelling Helps Reading

Sound out these words. Then read the story.

| | | | | | | |
|---|---|---|---|---|---|---|
| chart | march | star | bark | arm | barn | art |
| bore | core | fork | tore | torch | pork | fort |
| chore | horse | shore | thorn | stork | worn | short |
| cord | porch | wore | sport | horn | store | more |

"I am glad we gassed up and pumped up the tires, Art," said Mr. Archer. "We can drop off this load of corn at the store and still get some hard work done at the farm. See those dark clouds in the north? It may be warm, but I think a storm is coming up."

"I have some more chores, too," said Art. "Stop, Dad! See that warning on the bridge crossing the road? LOW BRIDGE, 12 FEET."

"Our large truck is at least an inch higher than 12 feet! We cannot force our truck through!"

"And there is no way to get by on the sides! Park the truck, Dad. The cars in back are starting to blow those horns at us."

"How in the world can we get by?" asked Mr. Archer.

"I have it," cried Art, jumping out of the truck.

What was Art's plan to get the truck under the bridge?

**A Pair of Square Steer Ear Words**

| fear | steer | fair |
| beard | peer | stairs |
| spear | dare | ▽ heart |
| tear | spare | ▽ tear |
| deer | stare | ▽ wear |

The words **pair** and **square** have the same vowel-r sounds.

We use the **air** and **are** spellings for the vowel-r sounds in **Pair** words and **Square** words.

The words **steer** and **ear** have the same vowel-r sounds.

We use **eer** and **ear** to spell the vowel-r sounds in **Steer** words and **Ear** words.

1. Write the **air** words. Draw a line under each **air**.

2. Say **dare**. Write **dare** and the other words with **are**.

*fear*    *deer*    *spare*    *heart*

*beard*    *steer*    *stare*    *tear*

*spear*    *peer*    *fair*    *wear*

*tear*    *dare*    *stairs*

**3.** Write the four **ear** words. Draw a line under each **ear**.

**4.** Write the **eer** words. Draw a line under each **eer**.

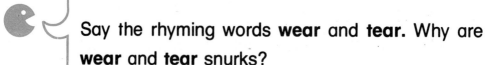

Say **heart.** Why do we call **heart** a snurk?

Say the rhyming words **wear** and **tear.** Why are **wear** and **tear** snurks?

**5.** Write the words for the pictures. Circle the snurk.

a.      b.      c.

**6.** Write the words that mean "pull in pieces" and "a drop of water from your eye."

**1.** Write the missing spelling words.

**a.** a _____ tire

**b.** a sharp _____

**c.** a large _____

**d.** curving _____

**e.** a fat _____

**f.** a torn _____

**2.** Each sentence has one wrong word. Write the sentences right.

Our dog fairs storms. He does not deer go out. He likes fear days.

**1.** Write **fear.** Change **f** to **cl** and to **r** and write the new words. Circle the word that means "back."

**2.** Write **deer.** Change **d** to **ch** and to **sn** and write new words. Circle the word that means "shout for joy."

**3.** Write **fair.** Change **f** to **p** and to **ch** and write new words. Circle the word that means "two of a kind."

**4.** Write **stare.** Change **st** to **b** and to **sc** and write new words. Circle the word that means "with no hair."

**5.** Add **ing** to **wear, tear,** and **peer.** Circle the word that means "looking."

**6.** Say **scare, pair, cheer,** and **wear.** Write the three words that rhyme.

**7.** Say **peer, sneer, stair,** and **deer.** Write the three words that rhyme.

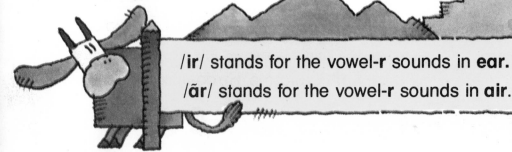

/ir/ stands for the vowel-r sounds in **ear.**
/ãr/ stands for the vowel-r sounds in **air.**

## Spelling Helps Reading

Sound out these words. Then read the story.

| | | | | | |
|---|---|---|---|---|---|
| share | rare | bare | ear | year | near |
| shear | snare | hair | beer | rear | clear |
| scare | care | air | cheer | hear | dear |

"Dad," cried Claire, "is that a hole in your sock? I dare say you tear up and wear out more than your fair share in one year! Why, you would go in your bare feet if Mom and I did not yell at you! Do you hear?"

"Have a heart," groaned Mr. Ware, who was dozing in a chair near the fire. "Cheer up and spare me your tears. Who cares? Who stares at my socks?"

"Mom and I do. Where are your clean socks?"

"All right," said Mr. Ware with a smile. "This gives me a chance to see how smart you are, Claire. In the drawer of my dresser I have six black and six brown socks, all mixed up. I need a pair that match. Run up the stairs and get them. You may not turn on the lights, so you will not see which are black and which are brown. Now, Claire, what is the least number of socks you can bring down to be sure that you have a matching pair?"

**What should Claire say?**

# 21　We'll Shrink Words

| | | |
|---|---|---|
| can't | I'll | o'clock |
| didn't | we'll | won't |
| isn't | I'd | don't |
| I'm | I've | couldn't |
| it's | let's | you're |

**We'll Shrink** words are **contractions**.

A contraction is a word that is made when we put two or more words together and leave out some of the letters.

We use an apostrophe to show where letters in a contraction are missing: **cannot—can't.**

**1.** Write the contractions for these words. Circle the snurks.

    **a.** did not      **b.** could not      **c.** is not

    **d.** I am      **e.** I have      **f.** you are

**2.** Write the contractions for these words.

    **a.** I will           **b.** I would           **c.** we will

> Say **do not** and **don't.** Do you hear the same vowel sound in **do** and **don't?**
>
> Say **will not** and **won't.** Do you hear the same vowel sound in **will** and **won't?**
>
> Why do we call **don't** and **won't** snurks?

**3.** Write the contractions for these words. Circle the snurks you write.

    **a.** do not           **b.** let us           **c.** will not

**4.** Long ago people said, "It is ten of the clock." Write **of the clock** and the contraction for **of the clock.**

## Working with the Word List

**1.** Write the contractions that mean the opposite of **can, did,** and **is.**

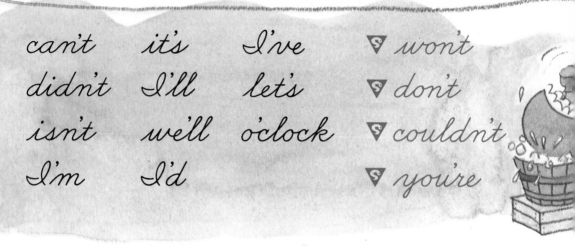

**2.** Write the two words that each of these contractions stands for.

    **a.** you're      **b.** I've      **c.** I'll

    **d.** isn't      **e.** didn't      **f.** let's

    **g.** I'd      **h.** we'll      **i.** I'm

**3.** Write the sentence. Use contractions for the words **we will** and **it is**.

    **We will** go swimming if **it is** not too cool.

**4.** Write the sentence. Use contractions for the words **I am** and **will not**.

    **I am** sure I **will not** drop them.

## Building Spelling Power

> We use an apostrophe to show missing letters in contractions.
> We also use an apostrophe to show owning.
>
> my friend's hat          a bear's tail

**1.** Write a contraction and another word with an apostrophe for each sentence.

**a.**          The ____ shoes ____ fit her.

**b.**          They ____ fix the ____ front tire.

**2.** Write the contractions for **could not**, **should not**, and **would not**.

**3.** Write the contractions for **I have**, **you have**, and **we have**.

 /v/ stands for the          sound that ends **I've**.

## Spelling Helps Reading

Say these contractions. Then read the poem aloud.

| | | | | | |
|---|---|---|---|---|---|
| shouldn't | hasn't | they're | you'll | she's | we've |
| wouldn't | hadn't | he'll | they'll | he'd | you've |
| haven't | doesn't | she'll | he's | she'd | that's |

Who thinks up ways for words to shrink?
Some printer who's run out of ink?
(I can't be sure—that's what I think.)

If I **will not**, I say "I won't."
If I **do not**, I say "I don't."
If I **could not**, I say "I couldn't."
If I **should not**, I say "I shouldn't."

We've **can't** and **didn't, I'd** and **I'm.**
(The ink they'll save won't cost a dime.)
We say "we'll send" and then "we've sent."
I say "I'll go," but not "I've went."
And we'll not say "one of the clock."
Let's shrink that down to "one o'clock."

So when we shrink our words, you see,
It is not (isn't) done for free.
The price is one **a-pos-tro-phe.**

108

# 22 Be-Bee Words

| | | | |
|---|---|---|---|
| be | blue | made | our |
| bee | blew | maid | hour |
| so | road | ▽ four | deer |
| ▽ sew | rode | for | dear |
| meat | sun | led | sea |
| meet | ▽ son | ▽ lead | see |
| ▽ your | weak | ▽ bear | |
| ▽ you're | week | bare | |

**Be-Bee** words are **homonyms.**

Homonyms are words that sound alike but have different spellings and different meanings.

to—too—two          eye—I
/tü/                        /ī/

**1.** Write 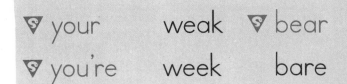 ,  , and

and the homonyms.

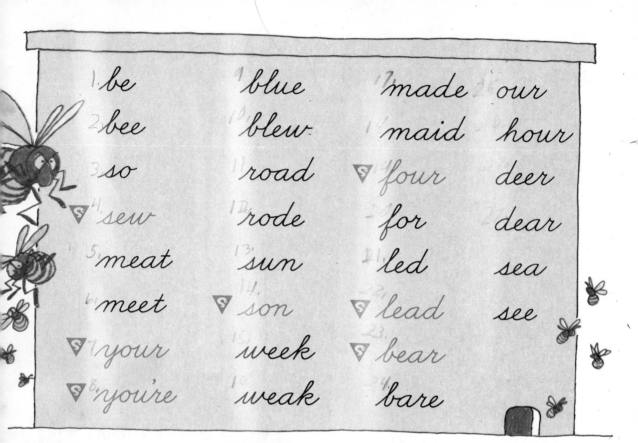

| be | blue | made | our |
| bee | blew | maid | hour |
| so | road | four | deer |
| sew | rode | for | dear |
| meat | sun | led | sea |
| meet | son | lead | see |
| your | week | bear | |
| you're | weak | bare | |

**2.** Write **4**, ☀, and ▇ . Then write the homonym of each word.

**3.** Write 🐻 , 👧 , and 🦌 . Then write the homonym of each word.

**4.** Write the words that mean "seven days," "from one o'clock to two o'clock," and "you are." Then write the homonym of each word.

**5.** Write the words that mean "stitch," "showed the way," and "look at." Then write the homonyms.

## Working with the Word List

**1.** Use five of these words to write a sentence. Remember to use the period.

them   do   He'll

four   her   for

**2.** Use five of these words to write a sentence. Remember to use the period.

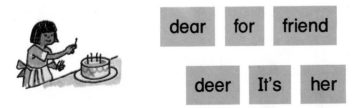

dear   for   friend

deer   It's   her

**3.** Use four words to write a sentence. Remember the period.

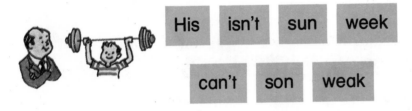

His   isn't   sun   week

can't   son   weak

111

## Building Spelling Power

**1.** Some words in the spelling list are nouns. Add **s** to these nouns to spell "more than one."

a.   b.   c.

**2.** Some words in the spelling list are verbs. Add **ing** to these verbs: **sew, see, be.**

**3.** Write the missing spelling words.

a.

They **ride** now.

They ___ then.

b.

The wind **blows.**

It ___ for an hour.

**4.** Write the "describing words" from the spelling list for these meanings.

a. much loved    b. not strong    c. with no hair

 /y/ stands for the sound that starts **your** and **you're.**

## Spelling Helps Reading

Say these homonyms. Then read the story.

| | | | | | | |
|---|---|---|---|---|---|---|
| to | buy | right | red | here | one | knew |
| too | by | know | read | there | won | would |
| two | write | no | hear | their | new | wood |

"Let's play that word game we thought up," said Ann. "We use spelling words and words in the Spelling Helps Reading list in sentences. The one who uses the most words from the two lists wins. Who has a sentence?"

"I'll get us started," said Dick, "but I've used just two words from the lists. This is it: **He knew he had read the book.**"

"I can beat that," cried Jane. "I used three words: **This meat will not stay fresh for more than an hour.**"

"I've got five in mine," said Paul. "This is it: **We'll buy two new blue suits next week.**"

"I have two more than you do, Paul," said Madge. "Hear this one: **No one will know the right place to meet if we don't write it down.**"

Can you write a sentence with more words from the Be-Bee lists than Madge used?

# 23 Way-Weigh Words

| | | | |
|---|---|---|---|
| weigh | fourth | tail | hole |
| way | forth | tale | whole |
| weight | cent | pail | heel |
| wait | sent | pale | heal |
| break | sail | eight | rain |
| brake | sale | ate | rein |
| through | herd | stare | |
| threw | heard | stair | |

**Way-Weigh** words are **homonyms.**

Homonyms sound alike but have different spellings and different meanings.

| way—weigh | hole—whole | forth—fourth |
|---|---|---|
| /wā/ | /hōl/ | /fôrth/ |

**1.** Write the homonyms with the /ėr/ sounds and the homonyms with the /ãr/ sounds. Circle the snurk.

**2.** Write the homonyms for the sound-spellings. Circle the snurks.

    **a.** /wā/        **b.** /hōl/        **c.** /fôrth/

    **d.** /rān/        **e.** /wāt/        **f.** /brāk/

**3.** Write the word for each picture. Then write the homonym under each word.

    **a.**            **b.**            **c.**

    **d.**            **e.**            **f.**

**4.** Write [image] and the five words that rhyme with [image] . Circle the word that means "not bright." Draw a line under the word that means "a story."

**5.** Write the homonyms with the /ē/ sound and the homonyms with the /e/ sound.

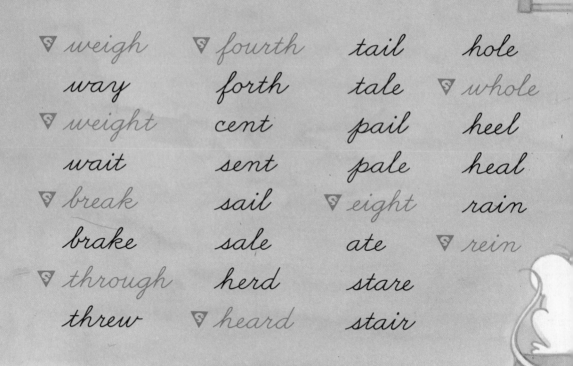

| | | | |
|---|---|---|---|
| ▽ weigh | ▽ fourth | tail | hole |
| way | forth | tale | ▽ whole |
| ▽ weight | cent | pail | heel |
| wait | sent | pale | heal |
| ▽ break | sail | ▽ eight | rain |
| brake | sale | ate | ▽ rein |
| ▽ through | herd | stare | |
| threw | ▽ heard | stair | |

## Working with the Word List

> Sound-spellings show how we say words.
> /brāk/ shows how we say **break** and **brake**.
> /brāk/ shows every sound in **break** and **brake**.

**1.** Write the homonyms for these sound-spellings.

    **a.** /thrü/       **b.** /stār/       **c.** /hėrd/

**2.** Write the words /fôrth/ and /hōl/ for the sentence.

The mouse crept _____ from its _____.

## Building Spelling Power

The first verb in each pair tells what we do "now." The second verb in each pair tells what we did "in the past": **think—thought, bring—brought, drink—drank.**

Write the "in the past" verbs for each "now" verb.

**1.** hear          **2.** send          **3.** throw

**4.** win          **5.** know          **6.** blow

**7.** eat          **8.** ride          **9.** buy

**10.** make          **11.** sell          **12.** draw

**13.** sink          **14.** break          **15.** meet

/w/ stands for the sound that starts **way** and **weigh.**
/h/ stands for the sound that starts **herd** and **heard.**

## Spelling Helps Reading

Say these homonym snurks.

| to | one | their | son | through | weigh |
| two | won | there | sew | whole | weight |
| buy | here | your | break | rein | four |
| would | fourth | you're | heard | eight | bear |

Read the story. Answer the questions at the end.

"Let's play that word game once more," said Jack. "This time we'll use all the homonyms we've had."

The class got to work. Mike O'Hare raised his hand.

"I used three: **He threw his weight on the brake.**"

"I have three, too," said Madge. **"The stag led the herd of deer."**

"I used four," said Fern. **"No one found the right way."**

"I used five," said Fred. **"Did you know there is a big one cent sale?"**

"I didn't count mine," said Kate, "but I think I'll win. This is mine: **I would like to buy four new blue pens for our dear friends to write with.**"

How many homonyms did Kate use in her sentence? Can you write one with more? Try.

**118**

# 24 Knock-Knee Words

| | | |
|---|---|---|
| knife | wrist | fright |
| knock | crumb | sign |
| knee | thumb | comb |
| wrong | chalk | half |
| wrap | taught | calf |

**Knock-Knee** words have silent consonant letters.

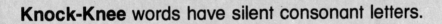

| | | |
|---|---|---|
| knee /nē/ | wrap /rap/ | crumb /krum/ |
| fright /frīt/ | chalk /chôk/ | half /haf/ |

1. Say the Knock-Knee words. Hear the sounds.

2. Write the words that start with silent **k** before **n**.

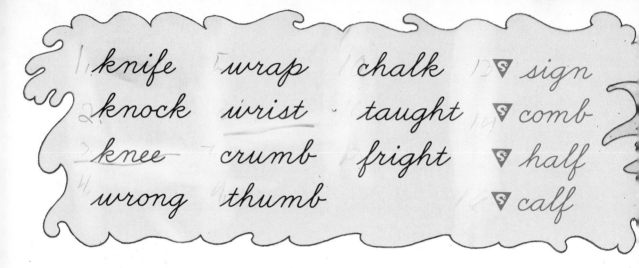

| knife | wrap | chalk | S sign |
| knock | wrist | taught | S comb |
| knee | crumb | fright | S half |
| wrong | thumb | | S calf |

**3.** Write the words that start with silent **w** before **r**.

**4.** Write the words that end with silent **b**. Circle the snurk.

**5.** Write **sign** and the words with silent **gh**. Circle the snurk. Draw a line under the word that means "a scare."

**6.** Write the words with silent **l**. Circle the snurks.

## Working with the Word List

**1.** Write the word for each picture. Circle the word that ends with the /m/ sound.

a.                    b.                    c.

**2.** Write the word for each meaning.

    **a.** not right        **b.** rap        **c.** a small,
                                                 small bit

**3.** Three words start with the /k/ sound. One starts with the /ch/ sound. Write the four words in alphabetical order.

> Say **pond, clock,** and **comb.**
> Why do we call **comb** a snurk?
>
> Say **silk, since,** and **sign.**
> Why do we call **sign** a snurk?

**4.** Write the four snurks in the spelling list. Draw a line under the words with the /a/ sound.

**5.** Write the sentence below. Use two of these words to fill the spaces.

    have     half     hole     whole

    A \_\_\_\_ peach is more than \_\_\_\_ of a peach.

**6.** Write the word for each picture.

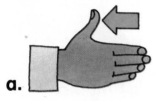
  **a.**

  **b.**

  **c.**

## Building Spelling Power

Write the sentences. Draw a line under each Knock-Knee word. Use capital letters and periods the right way.

1.

| climb | to | limb |
| don't | up | high | that |

2.

| come | tight | won't |
| this | loose | knot |

3.

| walk | the | through |
| snow | couldn't | John |

4.

| the | ought | hang |
| to | sign | straight |

/**m**/ stands for the sound that starts **made**.
/**m**/ stands for the sound that ends **thumb**.

## Spelling Helps Reading

Read these Knock-Knee words.

| | | | | | | |
|---|---|---|---|---|---|---|
| climb | fought | knot | light | should | weight | whose |
| could | kneel | know | night | straight | who | wreck |
| dumb | knelt | known | ought | talk | whole | write |
| eight | knew | lamb | right | walk | whom | wrote |

Write the word in each row that does not fit with the others.

1. climb     kneel     knit     know     dumb
2. wrong     talk     write     weigh     could
3. taught     two     caught     fought     wrote
4. knelt     knew     straight     thought     slept
5. ought     could     would     whole     should
6. knot     lamb     night     weight     two
7. knife     wreath     tight     crumb     wrist
8. thumb     calf     chalk     bought     sign

Put **g** and **h** in **through** and **right**
And **w** in **wrong** and **write**.
A **lamb** may **kneel** down on its **knees,**
So don't leave out those **k**'s and **b**'s.
A **calf** can **walk.** Don't sound the **l.**
But do not skip it when you spell.

# 25 Tiny Easy Words

dirty      cra zy      on ly

empty     ea sy      bus y

sil ly      ti ny      eve ry

sor ry    ang ry    ear ly

ug ly     hung ry   heav y

**Tiny Easy** words have two parts, or **syllables.**

In **Tiny Easy** words, the **y** at the end spells the /ē/ sound.

**1.** Say the Tiny Easy words. Hear the syllables. Hear the /ē/ sound at the end of each word.

**2.** Write the words in which the last syllable is **ly.** Circle the snurks.

**3.** Write the words in which the last syllable is **ty, sy, zy,** or **ny.** Draw a line under the last syllable in each word.

124

Say **every.** Hear the two syllables. The word **every** looks like a three-part word, but the **e** in the middle is silent.

**4.** Write **heavy** and **every.** Draw a line under the last syllable in each word. Circle the word that means "weighing a lot."

Say **angry** and **hungry.** Hear the syllables. We HEAR the /ng/ sound in the first syllable of **angry** and **hungry.**
We HEAR the /g/ sound in the second syllable. But we SEE only one letter **g.**

**5.** Write **angry** and **hungry.** Circle the word that means "wanting food."

## Working with the Word List

**1.** Write the word for each meaning.

    **a.** very small    **b.** not clean    **c.** not pretty

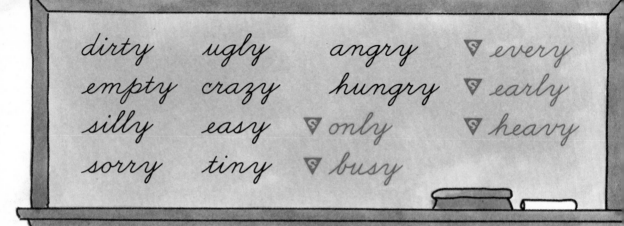

*dirty   ugly   angry   ▽ every*
*empty   crazy   hungry   ▽ early*
*silly   easy   ▽ only   ▽ heavy*
*sorry   tiny   ▽ busy*

**2.** Write the word for each meaning. Circle the snurks.

    **a.** hard at work    **b.** just one    **c.** not hard

> The Tiny Easy words tell how things look or feel. They are "describing words." We call them **adjectives.**

**3.** Write a Tiny Easy adjective for each picture.

  **a.**      **b.**      **c.**

**4.** The sentence has three mistakes. Write it right.

    every cat has a crasy hat

# Building Spelling Power

Say the Tiny Easy words. In each word the first syllable is loud and the second syllable is soft.

We use an **accent mark** to show the loud syllable.

ti ny  /tī′ nē/    ea sy  /ē′ zē/

Write the missing words. The sound-spellings tell you which words to write.

1. He's ____ he acted ____.

/sôr′ ē/        /sil′ ē/

2. Her ____ book is ____.

/tī′ nē/        /ē′ zē/

3. ____ dog was ____.

/ev′ rē/    /hung′ grē/

/z/ stands for the ████ sound in **crazy**.

| fancy | safety | jolly | icy | salty | loudly |
| truly | baby | simply | noisy | nearly | greasy |
| plenty | curly | thirsty | hardly | barely | slowly |

Read the story. Answer the question at the end.

"Have a busy day at the store, Daddy?" asked Nancy Hardy. "You're home early."

"Hardly," said Mr. Hardy slowly. "But I'm very angry. I had a dirty trick played on me, I'm sorry to say. A big, husky man bought a pair of heavy work shoes for $12. He handed me a greasy $20 bill. I had no change. Wally Tracy, whose candy store is next door, had plenty. He gave me twenty $1 bills. I gave the man eight $1 bills in change. The $20 bill was no good. I paid Mr. Tracy back. I'm out the $12 shoes, $8 in change, and the $20 I paid Tracy."

"You lost $40?" cried Mrs. Hardy. "That's not very funny."

"No, Betsy. I gave $8 to the man and $20 to Tracy. So I'm out only $28."

"You're both wrong," said Nancy.

How much did Mr. Hardy really lose?

128

# 26 Candy-Candies Words

can dy–can dies     jel ly–jel lies

cit y–cit ies         cop y–cop ies

pup py–pup pies    hob by–hob bies

po ny–po nies      pen ny–pen nies

bod y–bod ies      wor ry–wor ries

dair y–dair ies     cher ry–cher ries

cook y–cook ies    coun try–coun tries

ar my–ar mies

When words end in a consonant letter and
**y,** we change the **y** to **i** before we add **es.**

**1.** Say the **y**-ending words and their **es** forms.

**2.** Write the **y**-ending words that start with the /p/ sound.
After each word, write its **es** form.

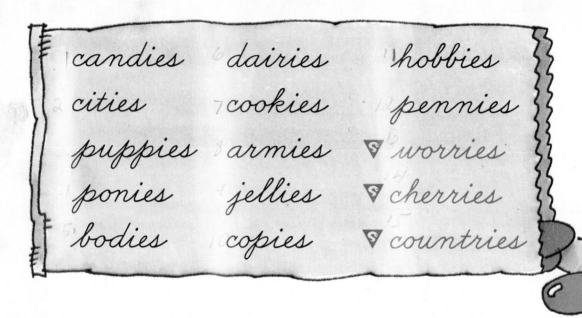

candies    dairies    hobbies
cities    cookies    pennies
puppies    armies    worries
ponies    jellies    cherries
bodies    copies    countries

**3.** Write the **y**-ending words that start with the /k/ sound. After each word, write its **es** form.

**4.** Write the **y**-ending word that starts with the /s/ sound. After the word, write its **es** form.

**5.** Write the **es** forms of **hobby, jelly, dairy,** and **army.**

**6.** Write the **y**-ending forms of **cities, bodies,** and **pennies.** Circle the word that means "one cent."

We use **or** to spell the /ôr/ sound in **fork,**
     **er** to spell the /èr/ sound in **her,**
     **ou** to spell the /ou/ sound in **out.**

Say **worry, cherry,** and **country.** Why do we call these words snurks?

**7.** Write the **y-ending** forms of the snurks. Circle the word that names a place.

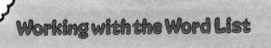
**Working with the Word List**

**1.** Write the word for each picture. Draw a line under the first syllable in each word you write.

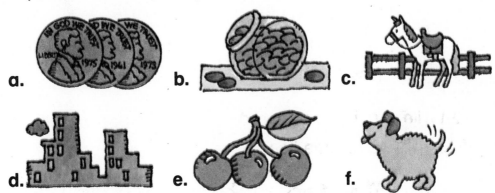

a.

b.

c.

d.

e.

f.

**2.** Use spelling words to fill the spaces.

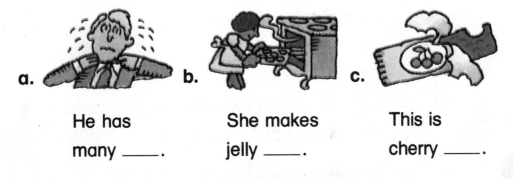

a.

b.

c.

He has
many ____.

She makes
jelly ____.

This is
cherry ____.

**3.** Use all the letters to write **y-ending** spelling words.

   **a.** byhob        **b.** yarm        **c.** raidy

**131**

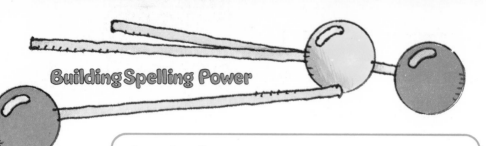

## Building Spelling Power

Say the Candy words. Hear the syllables. In each word, which syllable is loud—the first syllable or the second?

What do we call the mark that shows a loud syllable?

po ny /pō′ nē/     cop y /kop′ ē/

**1.** Write the missing words. The sound-spellings tell which words to write.

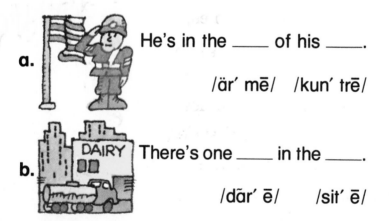

**a.** He's in the _____ of his _____.

/är′ mē/   /kun′ trē/

**b.** There's one _____ in the _____.

/dãr′ ē/     /sit′ ē/

**2.** The words **copy** and **worry** can be used as verbs. Change **y** to **i** and add **ed** to write the past forms of **copy** and **worry.**

/j/ stands for the sound that starts **jelly** and **jellies.**

Sound out these Candy-Candies words. Then read the poem.

| | | |
|---|---|---|
| story—stories | party—parties | county—counties |
| navy—navies | buggy—buggies | daisy—daisies |
| bunny—bunnies | thirty—thirties | twenty—twenties |
| fifty—fifties | forty—forties | sixty—sixties |

If you have nouns that end with **y**
That you would like to mul-ti-ply,
You will get more, and never less.
Just change the **y** to **i-e-s.**

Tell your stories, feed your puppies,
Ride your ponies, catch some guppies,
Go to parties, read the funnies,
Make some copies, pat your bunnies,
Bake your cookies, pick your cherries,
Eat your candies, cook your berries.
We get milk from cows in dairies,
Dimes and quarters from tooth fairies.

So tack **e-s** onto your penny
And you'll have not just one, but many.
Drop them in your piggy banks,
And when you're rich, send us your thanks!

133

# 27 Silver Dollar Mirror Words

| | | |
|---|---|---|
| sil ver | flow er | ▽ neigh bor |
| sis ter | dol lar | ▽ sug ar |
| but ter | cel lar | ▽ an swer |
| cor ner | doc tor | ▽ broth er |
| let ter | ▽ mir ror | ▽ a noth er |

In each **Silver Dollar Mirror** word, the soft syllable ends with a vowel letter and **r**.

**er** spells the vowel-r sounds in **silver.**

**ar** spells the vowel-r sounds in **dollar.**

**or** spells the vowel-r sounds in **mirror.**

**1.** Say the spelling words. Hear the syllables.

**2.** Write the words in which **er** spells the vowel-r ending. Circle the snurks.

134

**3.** Write the words in which **ar** spells the vowel-**r** ending. Circle the snurk.

**4.** Write the words in which **or** spells the vowel-**r** ending. Circle the snurks.

**5.** Write **brother, another,** and **answer.** Circle the word with a silent **w.**

**6.** Write the words **neighbor, sugar,** and **sister** in alphabetical order.

## Working with the Word List

**1.** Write the words for these meanings.

**a.** 100 pennies

**b.** bloom

**c.** one more

**d.** one who lives near

**e.** place where walls meet

**f.** room under ground

**2.** Write the word for each picture.

**a.**

**b.**

**c.**

silver    flower    neighbor
sister    dollar    sugar
butter    cellar    answer
corner    doctor    brother
letter    mirror    another

 Snurks have tricky spellings. Say the snurks. Look at the letters. Hear the sounds.

**3.** Write the snurks with these sounds in the loud syllables.

    **a.** /ā/          **b.** /sh/         **c.** /a/

**4.** Each sentence has a wrong word. Use spelling words in place of the wrong words. Write the sentences right.

    **a.**       Mother adds salt to make food sweet.

    **b.**       My brother likes better on his bread.

## Building Spelling Power

**1.** Add **or** to **sail, tail,** and **tract** to spell new words.

a.

b.

c.

**2.** Add **er** to **teach, check,** and **sweep** to spell new words.

a.

b.

c.

**3.** Use four of the new words you wrote. You must add **s** to two of the words.

a.

The two ＿＿ are

playing ＿＿.

b.

The ＿＿ is showing

the class a ＿＿.

/ŦH/ stands for the ✒ sound in **mother** and **brother.**

137

## Spelling Helps Reading

Sound out these Silver Dollar Mirror words.

| under | beggar | cedar | clever | ever | sailor | tractor |
| winter | actor | tailor | collar | farmer | tower | supper |
| whisper | author | better | dinner | harbor | teacher | paper |

Read the story. Talk over the answer to the question.

Elmer Miller was reading a letter from an older brother, Victor, to his sister Ann.

"Delmar Beecher, my neighbor, and I have been racing our motor boats in the river this summer," wrote Victor. "As I climbed down the rope ladder in the harbor, I slipped and got a bad sprain. Some sailor! Doctor Taylor said the limb will be better soon, so don't tell Father and Mother. Well, I'll run down to the corner and get this letter in the mail. Must hurry back in time for dinner. Love, Victor."

"That Victor!" cried Ann. "He didn't say which of his limbs he's sprained!"

"Use your head, Ann," said Elmer. "It was his left wrist, of course."

How did Elmer know?

# 28 Little People Words

| | | |
|---|---|---|
| lit tle | mid dle | ap ple |
| bot tle | tur tle | un cle |
| bub ble | han dle | whis tle |
| ta ble | nee dle | ▽ peo ple |
| can dle | a ble | ▽ trou ble |

In each **Little People** word,
the soft syllable ends with **le.**

**1.** Say the Little People words. Hear the two syllables.

**2.** Write the words that have these doubled consonant
letters: **dd, tt, pp, bb.** Draw a line under each soft syllable.

**3.** Write the words with **nd** and **rt.** Draw a line under each
soft syllable.

little    middle    apple
bottle    turtle    uncle
bubble    handle    whistle
table     needle    people
candle    able      trouble

**4.** Write  , and the word that rhymes with

. 

**5.** Write **uncle** and **whistle.** Draw a line under each soft syllable. Circle the word with a silent **t.**

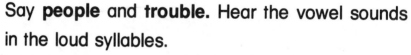

Say **people** and **trouble.** Hear the vowel sounds in the loud syllables.
Do we expect **eo** to spell the /ē/ sound?
Do we expect **ou** to spell the /u/ sound?
Why do we call **people** and **trouble** snurks?

**6.** Write the snurks. Draw a line under the word that means "worry or bother."

## Working with the Word List

**1.** Add **s** to Little People words to spell "more than one."

a.

b.

c.

d.

e.

f.

**2.** Three spelling words have the /i/ sound in the loud syllable. Write the /i/ words in alphabetical order.

**3.** The letters in these words are mixed up. Spell the words right.

    **a.** labe       **b.** cunel       **c.** poleep

**4.** Spell these words right.

    **a.** tebal       **b.** papel       **c.** dimdel

**5.** Write the words that begin with these sounds.

    **a.** /k/       **b.** /m/       **c.** /n/

 Nouns are "naming words." They name people or places or things.

| | | |
|---|---|---|
| brother | country | needle |
| sister | city | sugar |

**1.** Write new Little People nouns with doubled consonant letters.

 a.    b.    c.

 Adjectives are "describing words." They tell how things look or sound.

**little** child   **busy** people   **purple** cloth

**2.** Write **simple, nibble,** and **gentle.** Draw a line under each adjective.

**3.** Write an **le** adjective for each meaning.

**a.** easy        **b.** small        **c.** kind

 /n/ stands for the sound that starts **needle.**

142

## Spelling Helps Reading

Sound out these Little People words.

| | | | | | |
|---|---|---|---|---|---|
| ankle | circle | paddle | steeple | gobble | juggle |
| bundle | eagle | pickle | sparkle | simple | settle |
| cattle | gentle | wrinkle | puzzle | saddle | jungle |

Read the story and answer the question.

"It's simple, Billy," said Uncle Ben. "You mark a little circle on the maple tree. Whittle a hole and plug in a spout. Loop the handles over the spout. The sap trickles down and fills the pail. People bottle the sap, set it on their tables, and pour it on griddle cakes and waffles. We can boil it, too, to make sugar. Here, have a sample."

Uncle Ben dipped a ladle into one of the pails. Billy's eyes sparkled as he tasted the sweet sap.

"Now, Billy," chuckled Uncle Ben, "you can barely reach those pails, so you can help bring the sap in. The trees grow at least one foot each year. By next year you won't be able to reach the pails."

Billy looked puzzled. Then his eyes twinkled.

"Yes, I will. I'll be able to reach them next year, and the year after — and every year."

Why will Billy be able to reach the pails?

143

# 29 Inside Outside Words

in side      be long      good-by

out side     may be     in to

can not     near by     to day

for got     with out     no thing

be side     side walk    in stead

**Inside Outside** words are called **compound** words.

We form compound words by joining shorter words to make new words.

**in + side = inside    side + walk = sidewalk**

**1.** We spell compound words by looking at the shorter words and spelling them. Write the words that have **side** as one of the shorter words.

**2.** Write the compound words that have **be** as one of the shorter words. Circle the word that means "by the side of."

**3.** Put each pair of words together to form a compound word.

**a.** can   not      **b.** near   by      **c.** in   to

**d.** for   got      **e.** to   day      **f.** with   out

**g.** in   stead     **h.** no   thing    **i.** side   walk

Say **no** and **thing.** Then say **nothing.**
Why do we call **nothing** a snurk?
Why do we call **into, today,** and **instead** snurks?

**4.** Write **good-by, nothing,** and **instead.** Circle the compound that has a **hyphen,** or small line, between the shorter words.

## Working with the Word List

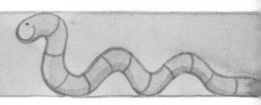

**1.** Use the words to tell what the girl said.

"_____," said Jo Ann.

| cannot | go | outside |
|--------|-----|---------|

| without | You | boots |
|---------|-----|-------|

145

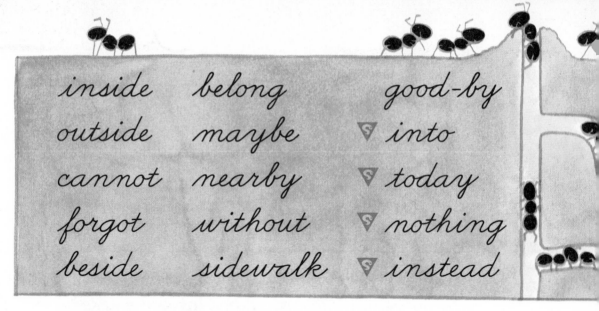

*inside*  *belong*  *good-by*
*outside*  *maybe*  *into*
*cannot*  *nearby*  *today*
*forgot*  *without*  *nothing*
*beside*  *sidewalk*  *instead*

**2.** Use the words to tell what the boy said.

Peter said, "_____."

| nothing | bundle | inside |
|---------|--------|--------|

| there | is | this | Maybe |
|-------|----|----|------|

**3.** Use two spelling words and two review snurks to fill the spaces. The sound-spellings tell you which words to use.

**a.** _____ makes him _____.

/nuth' ing/   /laf/

**b.** They _____ _____ to him.

/bōth/   /bē lông'/

146

# Building Spelling Power

**1.** Spell the new compound words.

a.

b.

c.

d.

e.

f.

**2.** Use the words in each box to spell two compound words.

a.
| base | air |
|------|-----|
| plane | ball |

b.
| boat | print |
|------|-------|
| sail | foot |

c.
| side | out |
|------|-----|
| with | walk |

/tü/ is how we say **to.** /dā/ is how we say **day.**

/tü dā′/ is how we say **today.**

 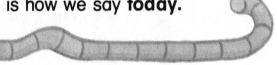 

**Spelling Helps Reading**

Sound out these compound words.

| | | | |
|---|---|---|---|
| airplane | cowboy | handlebars | stepladder |
| baseball | fingernail | horseshoes | tablecloth |
| butterflies | firemen | pancake | toothbrush |
| buttermilk | flowerpot | rainbow | waterfall |
| candlestick | football | sailboat | workman |

Write the word that does not belong in each row.

1. woodpecker    bluebird    peacock    reindeer
2. eyebrow    toothbrush    eardrum    kneecap
3. barnyard    grandstand    pigpen    woodshed
4. bookcase    fireplace    flashlight    footstool
5. snowsuit    raincoat    earmuffs    bathrobe
6. salesman    shortstop    goalkeeper    quarterback
7. butterfly    cockroach    sunfish    bumblebee
8. peanuts    popcorn    cheesecake    toothpaste
9. flagpole    fishhook    stickpin    thumbtack
10. redwing    greenhouse    bobwhite    sidewalk

Sing a song of sixpence, have a ham on rye—
Blackberry, blueberry, huckleberry pie!
You will have no trouble, if you play it smart—
Spot the compound pieces and spell them part by part!

# 30  Something Words

- some one
- some thing
- any one
- some time
- every thing
- your self
- every one
- grand father
- her self
- break fast
- grand mother
- him self
- any thing
- to morrow
- my self

**Something** words are **compound** words.

We put two shorter words together to form compound words.

We learn to spell compound words by looking at the shorter words and spelling them.

**some + thing = something**   **my + self = myself**

**1.** Say the Something words. Write the seven words that have **some** or **self** as one of the shorter words.

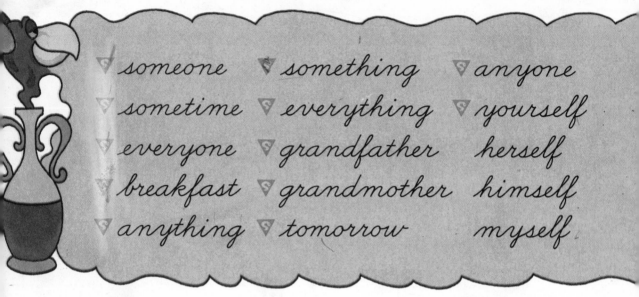

someone    something    anyone
sometime    everything    yourself
everyone    grandfather    herself
breakfast    grandmother    himself
anything    tomorrow    myself

**2.** Write the words that have **any** or **every** as one of the shorter words.

**3.** Write the words that have **grand, fast,** or **to** as one of the shorter words.

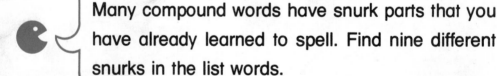

Many compound words have snurk parts that you have already learned to spell. Find nine different snurks in the list words.

**4.** Write the nine snurks that are in the compound words.

**5.** Write the three compound words that have no snurk parts.

# Working with the Word List

**1.** Write **grandmother** and **grandfather.** Circle the snurk part of each word.

**2.** Write the compound words with these meanings.

    **a.** a morning meal    **b.** the day after today    **c.** I or me

> We use a **comma** between **Yes** or **No** and the rest of a sentence.
>
>     Yes, I'll do it myself.
>     No, I don't want anything.

**3.** Use the words to write the **Yes** and **No** sentences.

**a.**
| to | going | Grandmother's |

| house | I'm | tomorrow | Yes |

**b.**
| his | hasn't | had | No |

| Grandfather | breakfast |

## Building Spelling Power

You have learned to spell **er**-ending words and **le**-ending words. Use an **er**-ending word or an **le**-ending word in each of these compound words.

1.

2.

3.

4.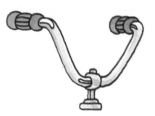

5.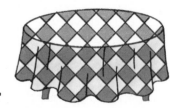

6.

/ev′ rē/ shows how we say **every**.

/hwãr/ shows how we say **where**.

What compound word does this sound-spelling stand for: /ev′ rē hwãr/?

## Spelling Helps Reading

Sound out these compound words.

| | | | |
|---|---|---|---|
| yesterday | toothbrush | playmate | peanut |
| everywhere | overcoat | newspaper | mailbox |
| highway | footprints | flashlight | haircut |
| bedroom | anybody | eyebrow | flagpole |
| anywhere | cardboard | birdhouse | airport |

Number your paper from 1 to 10. After each number, write **T** if you think the sentence is true. Write **F** if you think it is false. Be ready to tell why you gave the answer you did.

1. Everything you read in a newspaper headline is true.
2. Everyone is bound to do something wrong sometime.
3. Many people buy peanuts and popcorn at baseball games.
4. Football fans sometimes need waterproof raincoats.
5. Homeowners buy lawn mowers at hardware stores.
6. Chalkboards are useful in classrooms.
7. Everyone likes to eat grapefruit at breakfast.
8. Mailboxes make good birdhouses for bluejays.
9. Airplanes need runways to land at airports.
10. Farmers use pitchforks to make haystacks.

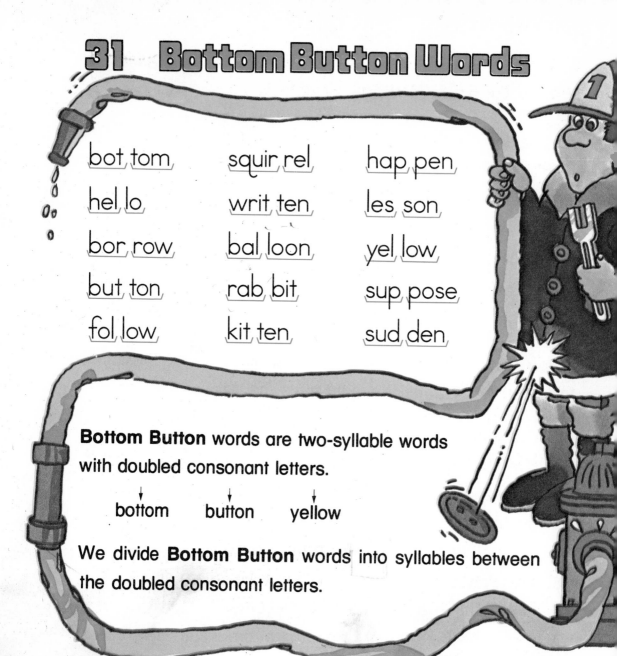

bot tom

hel lo

bor row

but ton

fol low

squir rel

writ ten

bal loon

rab bit

kit ten

hap pen

les son

yel low

sup pose

sud den

**Bottom Button** words are two-syllable words with doubled consonant letters.

bottom     button     yellow

We divide **Bottom Button** words into syllables between the doubled consonant letters.

**1.** Say the Bottom Button words. Hear the syllables.

**2.** Write the words with doubled **t** or doubled **p**. Draw a line under the first syllable in each word.

**3.** Write the words with doubled **r**, doubled **b**, or doubled **d.** Draw a line under the first syllable in each word that you write.

**4.** Write the words with doubled **l** or doubled **s.** Draw a line under the first syllable in each word.

**5.** Write the words for these meanings. Then say the words. Draw a line under each loud syllable.

  **a.** a toy made of    **b.** a greeting    **c.** think something
      thin rubber                              is true

**6.** Four words in the spelling list start with the /b/ sound. Write the /b/ words in alphabetical order.

**7.** Three words in the spelling list start with the /s/ sound. Write the /s/ words in alphabetical order.

## Working with the Word List

**1.** Write the word for each picture.

**a.**

**b.**

**c.**

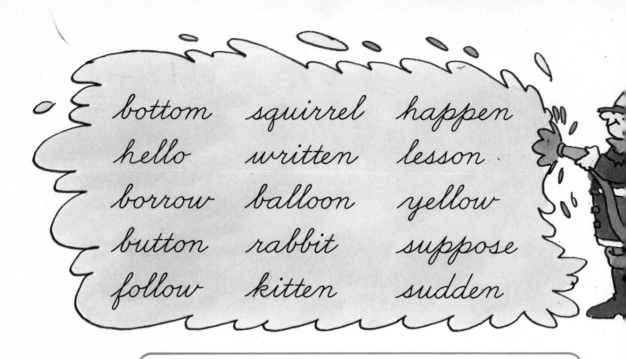

bottom   squirrel   happen
hello   written   lesson
borrow   balloon   yellow
button   rabbit   suppose
follow   kitten   sudden

> Two-syllable words are easy to spell if we look at each syllable and spell the words by parts.
>
> SAY **rabbit.**    SEE **rab bit**.
>
> Spell **rab** like a Fat Cat word.
>
> Spell **bit** like a Big Pig word.

**2.** Write the words that have these first syllables.

**a.** yel      **b.** les      **c.** kit

**d.** bot      **e.** fol      **f.** sup

**g.** but      **h.** sud      **i.** bal

**3.** Write the words that have the /ôr/ or /èr/ sounds in the first syllable.

Find the mistakes in the sentences. Write the sentences the right way.

**1.** Rabbits and kittens climb trees,

**2.** Yellow, brown, green, and purpel are collars.

**3.** Baloons are sometimes filled with ear.

**4.** "Hello," Said Betty. "I'm glad to meat you."

/hel′ ō/ shows one way to say **hello**.
/hel ō′/ shows another way to say **hello**.

## Spelling Helps Reading

Sound out these Bottom Button words. Then read the story.

| | | | | | |
|---|---|---|---|---|---|
| allow | traffic | arrow | attack | batter | tennis |
| swallow | banner | coffee | collect | hidden | common |
| chatter | hammer | inning | correct | narrow | quarrel |
| appear | manner | offer | pillow | ribbon | scatter |

On Saturday afternoon, Mr. Dutton was napping in his hammock in the late summer sun.

"Daddy," said Ellen, "aren't you going to paint my puppy's kennel?"

"Hello, Ellen," said her father, rubbing his eyes. "I suppose I can get it done tomorrow. You and Jimmy had better hurry and get the paint. Hammond's hardware store closes at six o'clock. Get a gallon of green paint."

"Sorry, young fellow," said Mr. Hammond to Jimmy. "It happens that I'm out of green. Got red, blue, and yellow, by the gallon and half gallon. No green, though."

"Oh, Jimmy," cried Ellen, "what can we do? Daddy will be out of town all next week!"

"Don't worry, Sis," said Jimmy with a smile. "You'll have a bright green kennel by Sunday night."

How did Jimmy plan to get the green paint?

**158**

# 32  Picnic Basket Words

| | | |
|---|---|---|
| pic nic | en joy | cir cus |
| pen cil | al so | in vite |
| un til | gar den | mar ket |
| bas ket | ex pect | mon key |
| win dow | al ways | al most |

**Picnic Basket** words are two-syllable words that have the vowel-**consonant-consonant**-vowel letter pattern.

    vc cv        vc cv

    pic nic      bas ket

We divide **Picnic Basket** words into syllables between the two consonant letters.

**1.** Say the Picnic Basket words. Hear the syllables.

**2.** Write the words that start with vowel letters. Draw a line under the first syllable in each word.

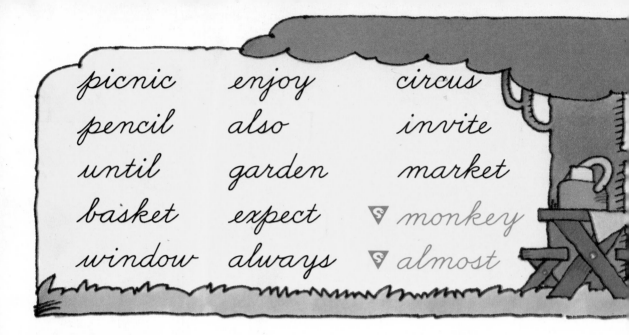

picnic     enjoy     circus

pencil     also     invite

until     garden     market

basket     expect     monkey

window     always     almost

**3.** Write the words that start with consonant letters. Draw a line under the first syllable in each word. Circle the snurk.

> Say **monkey.** Hear the vowel sounds in the syllables.
> Do we expect **o** to spell the /u/ sound?
> Why do we call **monkey** a snurk?

**4.** Write **pencil, window,** and **monkey.** Circle the word that has the /ng/ sound.

**5.** Write **picnic, circus,** and **almost.** Circle the word that has two /s/ sounds.

**6.** Write **invite, until,** and **circus.** Circle the word that has the /ī/ sound.

## Working with the Word List

**1.** Write the words for these meanings.

   **a.** too    **b.** be happy with    **c.** all the time

> Spell two-syllable words by parts.
> SAY **garden.**    SEE gar den.
> Spell **gar** like a Starch word.
> Spell **den** like a Red Hen word.

**2.** Write the words that have these first syllables.

   **a.** bas       **b.** cir       **c.** pen

   **d.** pic       **e.** in        **f.** win

   **g.** un       **h.** en       **i.** mar

**3.** Write the three words that have the /ô/ sound in the first syllable.

**4.** The letter **x** spells the /ks/ sound. Write the word that has the letter **x.** Write its **ing** and **ed** forms also.

# Building Spelling Power

Each sentence has two mistakes. Write the sentences the right way.

**1.** Everyone has gone two the Circus.

**2.** We expect to plant a garden in our back yarn,

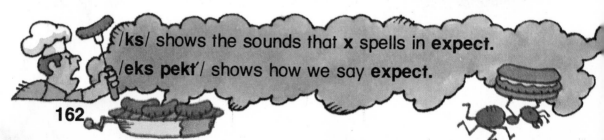

**3.** you should always put your pencil in you're desk.

**4.** Do you enjoy looking out off the window.

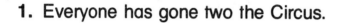

/**ks**/ shows the sounds that **x** spells in **expect**.
/**eks pekt**'/ shows how we say **expect**.

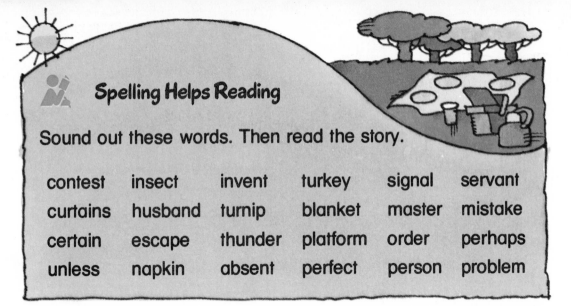

## Spelling Helps Reading

Sound out these words. Then read the story.

| | | | | | |
|---|---|---|---|---|---|
| contest | insect | invent | turkey | signal | servant |
| curtains | husband | turnip | blanket | master | mistake |
| certain | escape | thunder | platform | order | perhaps |
| unless | napkin | absent | perfect | person | problem |

"Perhaps your mother would enjoy perfume," said Mr. Lambert. "It makes a splendid birthday gift. A person seldom makes a mistake with perfume."

"That's a perfect answer to our problem, Arlene," said Norman. "How much, Mr. Lambert?"

"With the black velvet box, this bottle of perfume costs ten dollars. Tell you what I'll do. After Mrs. Denton has used up the perfume, bring back the bottle. I always show these lovely bottles in my store window. I'll pay you back the cost of the bottle. The perfume costs nine dollars more than the bottle."

"You mean we collect a dollar for the empty bottle?" asked Norman.

"That's not correct, Norman," laughed Arlene. "You need a number lesson."

Was Norman right? How much will Mr. Lambert pay?

# 33 About Alike Words

a•bout     a•live     a•lone

a•round    a•go     a•head

a•larm     a•wake     a•gain

a•like     a•part     a•bove

a•way     a•long     a•mong

**About Alike** words are two-syllable words that have the vowel-consonant-vowel letter pattern.

v  c v          v  c v          v  c v

a•bout          a•l i ke        a•part

We divide **About Alike** words into syllables before the consonant letter.

**1.** Write the words that have the word parts **round, long, part,** and **wake.**

**2.** Write the words that have the /ō/ sound in the second syllable.

**3.** Write the words for these meanings. Draw a line under the second syllable in each word.

    **a.** the same    **b.** not sleeping    **c.** not dead

    **d.** gone    **e.** once more    **f.** higher than

> Say **ahead, again, above,** and **among.**
> Do **ea** and **ai** usually spell /e/ as they do
> in **ahead** and **again?**
> Do **o**-consonant letter-**e** and **o** usually spell
> /u/ as they do in **above** and **among?**

**4.** Write the snurks. For each word, draw a line under the syllable that has the snurk spelling.

**5.** Write the four words **alarm, about, ago,** and **awake** in alphabetical order. Draw a line under the word in which two vowel letters spell one vowel sound.

**6.** Write the four words **among, apart, around,** and **alone** in alphabetical order. Draw a line under the snurk that you write.

**7.** Write the two words in the spelling list that end with a vowel sound.

*about  away  apart  § ahead*

*around  alive  along  § again*

*alarm  ago  alone  § above*

*alike  awake  § among*

## Working with the Word List

Write a spelling word for each space.

**1.** They're ____.

**2.** It's an ____.

**3.** He's not ____.

**4.** She's ____.

**5.** It goes ____.

**6.** It was long ____.

**7.** It's ___ cats.

**8.** It came ____.

**9.** He ran ____.

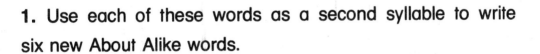

# Building Spelling Power

**1.** Use each of these words as a second syllable to write six new About Alike words.

    while     woke     loud     side     rise     mount

**2.** Write the sentences. Use periods and commas where they should be used.

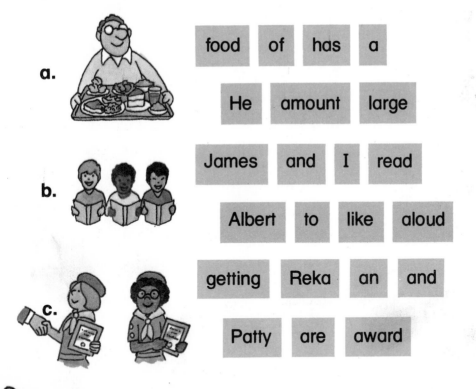

a.   food  of  has  a    He  amount  large

b.   James  and  I  read    Albert  to  like  aloud

c.   getting  Reka  an  and    Patty  are  award

/ī/ shows how we say **eye** and I.
We do not use capital letters in sound-spelling.

## Spelling Helps Reading

Sound out these V/CV words.
Then read the story.

| | | | | | |
|---|---|---|---|---|---|
| awoke | adult | amuse | award | ajar | amaze |
| avoid | adore | aside | ashore | adopt | arose |
| arise | aloud | awhile | amount | aboard | await |

When Homer Davis awoke, he arose and got dressed. Today was his birthday! Homer could hardly wait for the gift that came along every year from Grandfather Davis. His grandfather lived in another state, far away. Homer had not seen him since he was a year old, eight years ago. But Grandfather alone always knew what Homer wanted. This year, above all, Homer wanted a new first baseman's mitt.

And there on the breakfast table lay his gifts! Homer looked around among them for his grandfather's gift. He took it aside and opened it.

There it was! The mitt! But Homer's yell of delight turned into a groan when he tried it on.

"Don't be alarmed, Homer," said his dad. "We can trade the mitt in for another one."

**What was the matter with the mitt?**

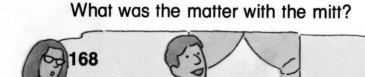

# 34 Parade Music Words

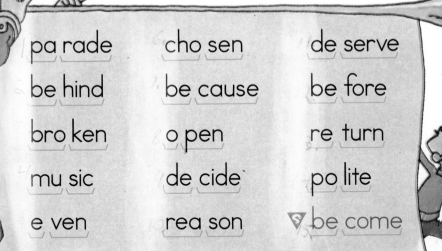

| | | |
|---|---|---|
| pa rade | cho sen | de serve |
| be hind | be cause | be fore |
| bro ken | o pen | re turn |
| mu sic | de cide | po lite |
| e ven | rea son | be come |

**Parade Music** words are two-syllable words that have the vowel-consonant-vowel letter pattern.

v cv          v cv

pa rade      mu sic

We divide **Parade Music** words into syllables before the consonant letter.

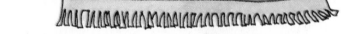

**1.** Say the spelling words. Hear the syllables.

**2.** Write the words in which the first syllable is **be**. Circle the snurk.

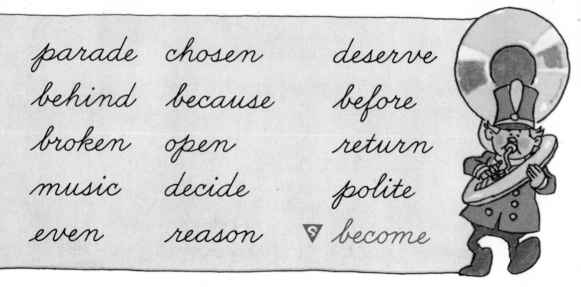

*parade* *chosen* *deserve*
*behind* *because* *before*
*broken* *open* *return*
*music* *decide* *polite*
*even* *reason* *become*

**3.** Write the three words with the /ō/ vowel sound in the first syllable.

In some of the Parade Music words, the first syllable is the loud syllable. In some of the words, the second syllable is loud.
The accent mark shows the loud syllable.

be hind'    rea'son    po lite'

**4.** Write **parade, behind, even,** and **reason.** Draw a line under each word in which the second syllable is the loud syllable.

**5.** Write **become, decide, deserve,** and **music.** Draw a line under each word in which the first syllable is the loud syllable.

**170**

**6.** Write **return.** Then write the **ed** and **ing** forms of the word **return.**

> V/CV words are easy to spell if we look at each syllable and then spell the words by parts.
>
> SAY **behind.**    SEE ‿be‿hind‿.
>
> Spell **be** as you spell **me** and **we** and **he.**
>
> Spell **hind** as you spell **find** and **mind.**

**1.** Write the words with these loud syllables.

a. ‿bro′‿___‿

b. ‿cho′‿___‿

c. ‿o′‿___‿

d. ‿rea′‿___‿

e. ‿e′‿___‿

f. ‿mu′‿___‿

g. ‿___‿rade′‿

h. ‿___‿lite′‿

i. ‿___‿fore′‿

**2.** Write an adjective, or "describing word," from the spelling list for each picture.

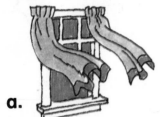

a.

b.

c.

# Building Spelling Power

**1.** Add **ly** to **even** and **polite** to spell new words. Say them. Hear three syllables in each word.

**2.** Each sentence has two mistakes. Find the mistakes. Write the sentences right.

**a.** Tommys painting was chosen as the beast.

**b.** Twelve drummer's are marking in the parade.

**c.** We have decided too move before winter begin.

Read this:  /bē kum′/  /iz/  /ā/  /snėrk/.

## Spelling Helps Reading

Sound out these V/CV words. Then read the story.

| | | | | | |
|---|---|---|---|---|---|
| began | protest | beneath | pilot | prepare | repair |
| direct | silent | final | spider | season | stolen |
| moment | below | motel | stupid | reward | pretend |

The pupils in Edith Mason's room decided to spend recess time telling stories and riddles. Edith was chosen to begin.

"Here's my riddle," she said. "Pretend that this high school band is playing music and marching in a parade before a football game. The students who play the drums march in a group. One drummer marches ahead of two drummers. One drummer marches between two drummers. And, finally, one drummer marches politely behind two drummers. What is the least number of drummers that belong in the band?"

The pupils were silent for a moment.

"There were nine drummers," cried David.

"No, there were five," said Suzy Dolan, who had been drawing drummers on a piece of paper.

**Who was right? How many drummers were there?**

# 35 Seven Minute Words

| | | |
|---|---|---|
| sev en | met al | giv en |
| sec ond | vis it | shad ow |
| pres ent | pun ish | min ute |
| fin ish | trav el | prom ise |
| wag on | or ange | mon ey |

**Seven Minute** words are two-syllable words with the VC/V letter pattern.

vc v          vc v          vc v

sev en        min ute        vis it

We divide **Seven Minute** words into syllables after the consonant letter.

**1.** Say the Seven Minute words. Hear the syllables. Write the words that start with the /m/ sound. Circle the snurk.

**2.** Write the words that start with the /s/ sound.

**3.** Write the words that start with the /p/ sound.

**4.** Write the words with these vowel sounds in the first syllable.

    **a.** /i/          **b.** /i/          **c.** /i/

    **d.** /i/          **e.** /a/          **f.** /a/

    **g.** /a/          **h.** /o/          **i.** /e/

Say **money.** What vowel sound does **o** spell in **money?** Why do we call **money** a snurk?

**5.** Write the snurks in this question: **Does your father have any money to give you?**

**6.** A "telling" sentence starts with a capital letter and ends with a period. A question starts with a capital letter and ends with a question mark. Unscramble these words to write a question. Then use the same words to write a true "telling" sentence.

seconds    seven    minutes    is

seven    than    longer

*seven*    *metal*    *given*

*second*    *visit*    *shadow*

*present*    *punish*    *minute*

*finish*    *travel*    *promise*

*wagon*    *orange*    *money*

## Working with the Word List

**1.** Write the words. Add **s** to spell "more than one."

a.    b.    c.

**2.** Write the words for these meanings.

   **a.** six plus one    **b.** next after first    **c.** end

**3.** The syllables in <u>vis el</u> and <u>trav it</u> are mixed up. The words should be **visit** and **travel.**

Write these mixed-up words right: <u>or ise</u>, <u>prom ange</u>.

176

## Building Spelling Power

**1.** Write the **ing** forms of **promise, finish,** and **punish.** Remember to drop the **e** before adding **ing.**

**2.** Write the sentences. Be sure to use a period at the end of each sentence.

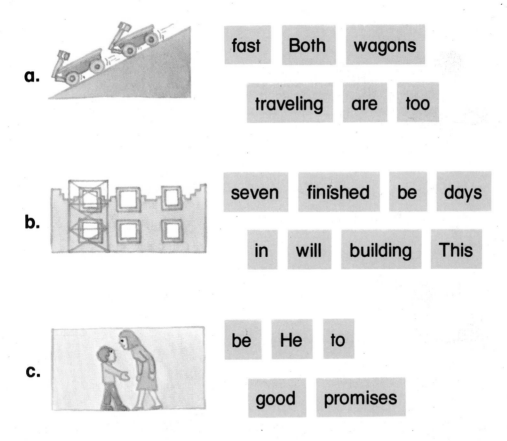

a.

| fast | Both | wagons |

| traveling | are | too |

b.

| seven | finished | be | days |

| in | will | building | This |

c.

| be | He | to |

| good | promises |

Read this: /fin′ ish/ /mēnz/ /end/.

177

**Spelling Helps Reading**

Sound out these VC/V words. Then write the right word to finish each sentence.

| vanish | cabin | figure | pedal | planet | record |
|--------|-------|--------|-------|--------|--------|
| spirit | damage | lemon | rapid | model | lizard |
| robin | driven | level | proper | manage | modern |

1. **Tree** is to **forest** as **robin** is to . . . .
   **a.** shower     **b.** birds     **c.** nest

2. **Second** is to **minute** as **inch** is to . . . .
   **a.** foot     **b.** width     **c.** size

3. **Tin** is to **metal** as **dollar** is to . . . .
   **a.** figure     **b.** penny     **c.** money

4. **Orange** is to **tree** as **berry** is to . . . .
   **a.** pie     **b.** petal     **c.** bush

5. **Lemon** is to **fruit** as **lizard** is to . . . .
   **a.** reptile     **b.** snake     **c.** mammal

6. **Travel** is to **wagon** as **fly** is to . . . .
   **a.** pedal     **b.** cabin     **c.** kite

7. **Timid** is to **bold** as **rapid** is to . . . .
   **a.** slow     **b.** foolish     **c.** limit

8. **Level** is to **even** as **clever** is to . . . .
   **a.** modest     **b.** stupid     **c.** smart

# 36 Surprise Words

| | | |
|---|---|---|
| sur prise | ex claim | king dom |
| com plete | help less | thir sty |
| hand ful | thank ful | ad dress |
| sand wich | hun dred | pump kin |
| chil dren | ex plain | ex tra |

**Surprise** words are two-syllable words with the VCCCV letter pattern.

| vc ccv | vc ccv | vcc cv |
|---|---|---|
| sur prise | hun dred | pump kin |

We divide some VCCCV words after the first consonant letter.

chil dren

We divide some VCCCV words after the second consonant letter.

pump kin

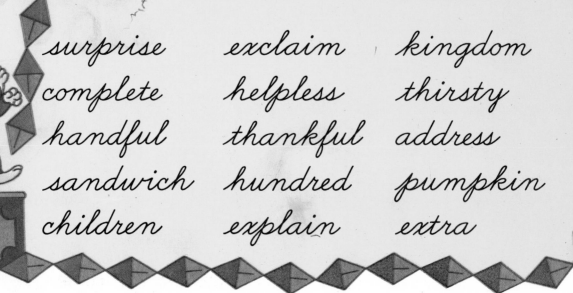

surprise     exclaim     kingdom

complete     helpless     thirsty

handful     thankful     address

sandwich     hundred     pumpkin

children     explain     extra

**1.** Write the words that start with the /h/ sound. Draw a line under the first syllable in each word. Circle the word that means "not able to do anything."

**2.** Write the words that are divided after the first consonant letter in the VCCCV letter pattern.

**3.** Write the words that are divided after the second consonant letter in the VCCCV letter pattern.

**4.** Write all the snurks in this question: **Does "extra" have two vowel letters?**

## Working with the Word List

**1.** Write the words that begin with a vowel sound.

**2.** Write a word for each of these starting sounds.

    **a.** /s/         **b.** /s/         **c.** /ch/

    **d.** /p/         **e.** /k/         **f.** /k/

    **g.** /th/        **h.** /th/       **i.** /a/

> Say **extra.** Hear the syllables.
> The **a** at the end of **extra** spells a new vowel sound.
> We show the new vowel sound like this: /ə/.
> We call /ə/ a **schwa.**

**3.** Write the words that start with **ex.** Circle the word that ends with the /ə/ sound.

**4.** Write the words for these pictures.

    **a.**              **b.**             **c.**

**5.** Write the words for these meanings.

    **a.** whole      **b.** something not   **c.** without help
                          expected

# Building Spelling Power

Write the right words.

**1. helpful** or **helpless?**

**2. pump** or **pumpkin?**

**3. child** or **children?**

**4. dress** or **address?**

**5. thirsty** or **thirty?**

**6. explain** or **exclaim?**

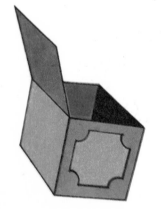

Read these sentences:

/spel' ing/   /helps/   /rēd' ing/.

/rēd' ing/   /helps/   /spel' ing/.

182

### Spelling Helps Reading

Sound out these VCCCV words.

| | | | | |
|---|---|---|---|---|
| although | complain | orchard | simply | partner |
| ostrich | control | handsome | instant | athlete |
| complain | entrance | hamster | laundry | farther |
| improve | darkness | antlers | concrete | explore |

Write each scrambled sentence correctly on a sheet of paper.
Then tell whether the sentence is **true** or **false.**

1. make pets hamsters good.
2. very birds are handsome ostriches.
3. hardware pickles are stores sold in.
4. improve athletes try their skills to good.
5. in laundries to work not people allowed are.
6. concrete made all sidewalks are of.
7. grown orchards in oranges and apples are.
8. seldom they sell merchants complaints get goods about.
9. stands at hundreds dog hot sandwiches of children purchase.
10. pumpkin turkey pie and remind the Pilgrims of us.

That's all
Till next fall.

# Spelling Consonant Sounds

/b/ ball

/d/ dog

/f/ fish

/g/ girl

/h/ hat

/l/ lamp

/m/ moon

/n/ nail

/p/ pig

/r/ rabbit

/t/ turtle

/v/ vase

# Spelling Consonant Sounds

**/w/** wagon

**/y/** yo-yo

**/z/** zebra

**/k/** black cat kite

**/j/** large fudge jar

**/s/** sun city

**/ks/** box

**/kw/** queen

**/hw/** wheel

**/ch/** rich witch

**/ng/** pink wing

**/sh/** ship

**/th/** **/ᵀH/** three feathers

# Spelling Vowel Sounds

**/a/** Fat Cat

**/e/** Red Hen

**/i/** Big Pig

**/o/** **/ô/** Hot Dog

**/u/** Rug Bug

**/ā/** Play Train Game

**/ē/** See Me Eat

**/ī/** Find My Fine Bright Tie

**/ō/** No Old Show Boat Smoke

**/ū/** **/ü/** Cute New Blue Suits

**/ou/** Loud Crowd

**/oi/** Toy Noise

# Spelling Vowel Sounds

/ô/
Maud's
Small Shawl

/u̇/
Good Book

/ü/
Cool Goose

/är/
Barn Yard

/ãr/
Hair Care

/ėr/
Her Girl Curl

/ir/
Hear Cheer

/ôr/
More
Short Boards

/ə/
About
Taken
Lemon
Pencil
Circus

## SOFT ENDINGS

/əl/
Final
Nickel
Pickle
Pistol

/ər/
Better
Color
Collar

/ē/
Tiny
Turkey

The following list contains the snurks that appear in the 36 units of this book. The numeral following each word shows the unit in which the snurk appears.

| | | | | |
|---|---|---|---|---|
| above 33 | comb 24 | half 24 | paste 13 | though 17 |
| again 33 | couldn't 21 | heard 23 | people 28 | thought 17 |
| ahead 33 | countries 26 | heart 20 | pour 17 | through 17 |
| almost 32 | country 26 | heavy 25 | prove 10 | today 29 |
| among 33 | course 17 | instead 29 | proving 10 | tomorrow 30 |
| another 27 | dead 7 | into 29 | quiet 5 | touch 17 |
| answer 27 | don't 21 | lead 22 | rein 23 | tough 17 |
| anyone 30 | early 25 | learn 18 | rough 17 | trouble 28 |
| anything 30 | earn 18 | lose 10 | search 18 | truth 14 |
| bear 22 | earth 18 | losing 10 | sew 22 | waste 13 |
| become 34 | eight 23 | love 10 | shove 10 | wear 20 |
| bought 17 | every 25 | loving 10 | shoving 10 | weigh 23 |
| bread 7 | everyone 30 | mirror 27 | sign 24 | weight 23 |
| break 23 | everything 30 | money 35 | someone 30 | whole 23 |
| breakfast 30 | fought 17 | monkey 32 | something 30 | wild 8 |
| brother 27 | four 22 | most 9 | sometime 30 | won't 21 |
| brought 17 | fourth 17 | neighbor 27 | son 22 | world 19 |
| busy 25 | front 1 | none 9 | soup 17 | worries 26 |
| calf 24 | grandfather 30 | nothing 29 | sugar 27 | worry 26 |
| cherries 26 | grandmother 30 | once 12 | sure 4 | worse 19 |
| cherry 26 | great 6 | only 25 | taste 13 | your 22 |
| child 8 | group 17 | ought 17 | tear 20 | you're 21 |